# "Imitate Me"

*From Paul to Timothy to Today:*
*The Timeless Model for*
*Spiritual Reproduction*

JAY BAKER AND
DAVE RATHKAMP

*To the beloved memory of Joe Coggeshall,*
*a true and faithful warrior for Jesus Christ,*
*whose devotion and selfless investment*
*in our lives continues to bear*
*fruit that remains.*

# Table of Contents

# Goal of "Imitate Me"

*"I hope in the Lord Jesus to send Timothy to you soon,
that I also may be cheered when I receive news about you.
I have no one else like him, who takes a genuine interest
in your welfare. For everyone looks out for his
own interests, not those of Jesus Christ.
But you know that Timothy has proved himself,
because as a son with his father he has served
with me in the work of the gospel."
(Philippians 2:19-22)*

Timothy, the young man the apostle Paul was discipling, had been fearful and lacked understanding when they started meeting. Although a true believer in Jesus Christ, Timothy sensed he had much to learn. Hesitantly, and with some understandable trepidation, Timothy began his spiritual relationship with Paul, the former zealot and Pharisee once known as Saul who had undergone a dramatic transformation himself.

After Timothy had studied, learned, absorbed, understood and matured in his faith under his teacher's direction, Paul sent him forward, initiating him into personal ministry to spread the Gospel of Jesus Christ. Thus entrenched and enriched, sending his Timothy was like Paul sending himself. Timothy was able to "imitate" Paul.

This amazing relationship between Paul and Timothy serves as one of the very best examples in the New Testament of one person discipling another. For that reason, we often refer to the discipler (or disciplemaker) as the "Paul" and the one being discipled as the "Timothy."

The focus of this book is to explore how the apostle Paul worked with Timothy, and how like-minded Pauls can become engaged in bringing men to full maturity. The book's goal is to help a Paul, or anyone interested in the one-on-one discipleship process, understand more fully all aspects of man-to-man ministry, the growth of one individual, and what the process of spiritual transformation looks like.

Throughout this book we offer principles and stories that can illustrate the modeling process that changes the life of a man: Timothy.

# Acknowledgements

For their involvement in the conception, writing and editing of this book, we want to express our appreciation to:

Our wives who supported our efforts to write this book: Nancy Baker, who typed the original draft from our often-unreadable hand-written notes, and Donna Rathkamp, who offered many helpful suggestions.

Tom Sawyer, who first suggested that this book needed to be written and offered many helpful ideas.

Sincere thanks are due for those who gave us permission to use their stories.

Patty Parr, who did the first editing and pointed us in the direction we needed to go with this topic.

Donna Redd, for the first draft proofreading.

Gary Cutbirth, Andy Schreck, Tom Muncey, Brandon Burk, David Ward and Jan Pound, for their insightful comments.

Laura Bower, for sharing her invaluable book writing and publishing perspectives.

The men who wrote their Timothy stories, and to Kim Cosco, for providing printing and publishing expertise.

Laura Starling, for her photography.

Bob Tamasy, for his professional expertise in the editing process.

Thank you!

# Foreword

...................

"This book shares with great transparency the broken lives of many men who have allowed God to transform their lives through His Word with the help of their Paul (or mentor) in a one-on-one discipleship relationship. Having been involved in the discipleship process for more than twenty years, I see tremendous value and encouragement in sharing certain chapters with my Timothy (or man being mentored) when he is struggling with similar issues. The chapter on 'Leadership in the Home' will give my Timothy a perspective he probably has never experienced before."

*(Randy Beck, Estate Planning Attorney, Houston, Texas)*


"Dave and Jay present a very unique view of discipleship – in fact, so unique it is much like that of Jesus Christ. 'Learning Not to Teach' was a pivotal chapter for me. As a Paul who wants to be a more effective discipler of men, I will be studying and making application of this book for many years to come – the insights are rich, unique and compelling!"

*(Robert J. Ketterer, President,*
*Visionworks Consulting, Atlanta, Georgia)*


"Even though running a business is often challenging, I find discipling a man one-on-one very humbling and yet completely rewarding. While it is critical to depend on the Holy Spirit in the discipling process, *Imitate Me* offers great spiritual and practical wisdom. I highly recommend this book to anyone, whether it is someone considering one-on-one discipleship or one that has discipled men for years."

*(Terry Looper, Founder and CEO, Texon LP, Houston, Texas)*

*"Imitate Me* illustrates vividly, through stories and life/Biblical principles, what it means to 'do life together' in a Paul-Timothy relationship. Highly recommended for those who want to get serious about 'making disciples who make disciples.'"

*(Mike Marker, Real Estate Developer and*
*Investor, Cincinnati, Ohio)*

"This book is an assemblage of wisdom gained from over 30 years in the real life trenches of one-on-one discipleship of businessmen; I know of nothing else like it anywhere. As a businessman who has been discipled and now disciples others, I have found *Imitate Me* a treasure trove of insights and lessons learned from actual experience that I both value highly and will use often. A wise friend once said to me, 'You can get experience the hard way by making your own mistakes, or the wise way, by gleaning from those who have gone before you.' That is exactly what this book provides. As such it is an invaluable resource to anyone desiring to answer the call of God to make disciples."

*(Kevin Ring, CEO of Trinity Development Company,*
*Sacramento, California)*

# Preface

It was author, poet and philosopher Henry David Thoreau that wrote, "The mass of men lead lives of quiet desperation." How well I have known desperation; it has met me many mornings as soon as I awake. Business has been slow the past couple of years. Yet I have to constantly remind myself not to get lost in routines centered on my business pursuits. Even weekends are disrupted because I no longer regard the time off as a valuable way to recover from a busy week. The point is, when business is good, I can easily lose myself in it. When it is bad, I find myself fighting feelings associated with desperation.

In his popular book of years ago, *The Road Less Traveled,* psychiatrist and author M. Scott Peck asserts that the number one rule a healthy person must accept is the premise that life is difficult – and to learn to act accordingly. This clearly resonates with me. A seasoned veteran of the difficulties of life, I've learned that if I accept Peck's advice, then when life's waves come crashing in on me, I must learn to ride the tide, somehow, some way.

Desperation and difficulty have been two of my closest and most loyal companions. This morning I felt compelled to write about them, hoping I would be enlightened and feel peace. It may be working.

A number of years ago I met a man who had overcome the desperation and difficulties of life and declared that he was not only *at* peace, but could *offer* peace. This man actually lived "in" another man, in a spiritual sense. Jesus, the Spirit, lived in the flesh and blood of a man named Dave, who had met Jesus through another man, Joe, who met Jesus through Pete, who met Jesus through Dan. I have no idea who it was that introduced Pete to Jesus, but I am confident it was another man.

Over the years, Jesus has become my truest, most reliable companion, and I have introduced Him to other men. In my world, imparting the life of Jesus to another man is commonly referred to as one-on-one discipleship. Discipleship is a process of sharing with another person the life of Christ dwelling inside you, a lifelong, day-by-day process. Once we start on the journey (of being a follower of Christ), life with Christ will last for eternity.

Jesus claims He has overcome the world (John 16:33) and defeated the devil. My battle is with me, the sinful "flesh man." This flesh man is the source of much of my struggle and suffering with life's desperation and difficulties.

This past week I heard stories of two Christian men who committed suicide. The thoughts of suicide have occasionally crossed my mind over the years as I wrestled with desperation and difficulties. Despite being painfully aware that life is not easy, I remain convinced that somehow Jesus living in me will work things out for my good (Romans 8:28).

There is a war going on within me daily. It is the same war that I believe all men live with, their own battles of quiet desperation. Jesus is my hope, as I am a prisoner of his hope (Zechariah 9:12). The only weapons I have in my battle – against the world, Satan, and my flesh – are the promises of Jesus (2 Corinthians 10:3-5). In this war I am determined to stand on the promises of my Lord God Jesus.

Peter was talking with the Lord in Luke 22. Jesus had just informed Peter that Satan had asked for permission that he might "sift (Peter) as wheat." Jesus assured Peter that He had prayed for him, that his faith would not fail, and when he returned from this time of "sifting" that he would go and strengthen his brothers. We can see in John 6:66 that when Jesus' teachings seemed too hard, many people decided to turn and walk with him no more. Jesus' list of those that disqualify themselves in this manner is a long one.

Inevitably, spiritual warfare will be encountered by those who go forward with their desire to help others come into God's Kingdom and grow to maturity. Because of the spiritual battles we all must engage in, it is critical to have strong relationships that are rooted in deep commitments to one another. It takes committed teams to accomplish the labor of making true disciples. The deeper the commitment to winning and discipling others, the more active and determined Satan, our spiritual enemy, is in fighting against us tooth and nail. In particular, he attacks our family members, wives, and children. It is important therefore to remain connected with those who can pray, offer comfort and provide support during times of trial.

"*Imitate Me*" is about the men who deal with life's difficulties by being involved in a Biblically based process. This movement of which they are a part centers on this global process –disciplemaking, an act of obedience that the Lord Jesus, in Matthew 28:19-20, has called us to in His Great Commission. – *Jay*

# Introduction

·······························

*"For even if you had ten thousand others to teach you*
*about Christ, you have only one **spiritual father**. For I became*
*your father in Christ Jesus when I preached the Good*
*News to you. So I urge you to **imitate me**."*
*(1 Corinthians 4:15-16, New Living Translation)*

The focus of this book is how one man, acting as Paul did, helps lead men to full maturity. It is written to assist a Paul, or anyone interested in the one-on-one discipleship process, to more fully understand the many aspects of man-to-man ministry, the growth of one individual man, and what true spiritual transformation looks like. The principles and stories we've incorporated here illustrate the modeling process that God uses to change the life of a man.

A story sometimes told about courageous Confederate General "Stonewall" Jackson illustrates the impact of leadership and modeling. During the Civil War, General Jackson led his men into battle riding his horse at the front of the charge. In one battle his horse was shot out from under him three times. Each time he got on another horse and went back to the battle, inspiring his men to "imitate him," to not quit, and to take the fight to the enemy.

The apostle Paul, himself a courageous leader, encouraged the Corinthian believers to "imitate me" in 1 Corinthians 4:16. Years before he made this statement, Jesus had called Paul to Himself on the road to Damascus, radically changing Paul's life from a zealous enemy of Jesus to a fervent, outspoken follower.

Ananias and Barnabas, both believers, influenced Paul as he was transformed and equipped to take the Gospel to the Gentiles. He traveled about his world from town to town, enduring suffering and great hardship, yet never losing his focus of starting ministries and discipling men. (2 Corinthians 11:23-27) Paul would spend several years in a town living with converts and supporting himself as a tentmaker.

The idea of "imitating" Paul's missionary lifestyle may seem impractical to most of us because we have jobs, homes, wives, children, aging parents and financial obligations. But we are writing – and appealing – primarily to those laymen who have, or will, take up this difficult calling to disciple men one-on-one, where they live and work (1 Corinthians 7:24). They are "modern day" Pauls, imitating the apostle's calling to model his life. Travel was Paul's way of teaching and spreading the Gospel. However, our way can be as convenient as staying right where we are and striving to be Paul-like in our own situations, entrusting what we learn from the Scriptures to reliable men who in turn pass it on to other reliable men. (2 Timothy 2:2)

The Church – the body of Christ – today is under attack from the culture, just as the Corinthian church had to function in a culture that was wicked, sexually immoral, unscrupulous with business dealings, and infected with corrupt pagan practices. How is a believer to live in this kind of environment? He needs a spiritual father who is more experienced. He needs a man standing alongside him during hard times. Ideally this is a man who likewise had a spiritual father who raised him up in the wisdom of Christ. With this kind of encouragement, nurture and support, some day the believer can impart this wisdom to his own spiritual son.

Local congregations and clusters of believers today desperately need present day Pauls in their own venues to fulfill the responsibility of the "spiritual father." Many churches today have ignored this teaching of Paul and give preference to teaching discipleship in a classroom, group setting, or from the pulpit. Today's churches often are filled with teachers, yet the discipleship process is not about instruction; it's about modeling a lifestyle. Discipleship is caught, not taught. It is created man-to-man in a relationship, where it is modeled: life-on-life in the flesh. We address the need of the body of Christ in the 21$^{st}$ century to return to Paul's example by modeling a proven process – first demonstrated in the first century – that will result in lives being changed forever.

What does it mean in 1 Corinthians 4:15 to have a spiritual father? Paul had birthed many of the Corinthian believers into Christ Jesus by the power of the Holy Spirit when they believed and received the Good News. Then he raised them up as his spiritual children. The new followers of Christ looked to Paul to provide wisdom for living life as a follower of Christ.

Biological fathers model for their children, and so do spiritual fathers. The disciples observed Jesus praying (Luke 11:2-4) and asked if He would teach them to pray. In response, He modeled praying what we know as the Lord's Prayer. Modeling usually precedes the teaching, as we can see in this example. It creates curiosity and a desire to learn, as opposed to projecting ourselves in the flesh onto others before they are ready to learn. The disciples learned to imitate Jesus as they began praying to the Father as they had observed Jesus praying.

Paul's relationship with Timothy is one excellent example of Paul teaching his spiritual son to "imitate me." This relationship between three people – Jesus, a Paul, and his Timothy – is one that, from time to time, we will refer to as "the JPT relationship." Jesus leads Paul and Timothy as they spend a great deal of time together in the discipleship process.

The apostle Paul's Timothy was fearful and lacked understanding when the two first started meeting. After Timothy observed, studied, learned, absorbed, understood and matured, Paul sent him forward, into the battle. At that point, sending Timothy was like Paul sending himself. Timothy was able to "imitate" Paul.

In Philippians 2:19-22 Paul states: *"I hope in the Lord Jesus to send Timothy to you soon, that I also may be cheered when I receive news about you. I have no one else like him, who takes a genuine interest in your welfare. For everyone looks out for his own interests, not those of Jesus Christ. But you know that Timothy has proved himself, because as a son with his father he has served with me in the work of the Gospel."*

Paul was given his charge by Jesus Christ, and we are given the same charge by Him to "go and make disciples of all nations" in Matthew 28:19-20. Since we are writing about going and making disciples in the current age, let's see how *today's* "Paul" is handling himself in this culture. What is it like for Paul to be with Timothy, and what would he be saying about life and following Christ in today's culture? To shed light on this, we and others will also write to you, the reader, as *today's* Timothy, sharing our stories with the discipleship process in the contemporary setting.

To clarify our role with the man we are discipling, we will often be writing using the name Paul. Our real names, of course, are not Paul. We are using his name because the apostle Paul of the Bible, 2,000 years ago, encouraged us to "imitate him" and that is what we have been doing and are describing for the readers (1 Corinthians 4:15-16). Therefore we ask that you give us the liberty of using Paul's name as if it were ours.

We are businessmen. Our experiences are reflective of discipling of other businessmen. We are writing with the idea that business and professional men would be the primary readers. Therefore, terms we use would indicate that the process described is man-to-man. The Bible offers no evidence that the apostle Paul ever discipled any women.

It is our experience that the discipleship process and spiritual parenting of woman-to-woman have differences in the way the relationships are established and worked out, but not in their content. A woman disciplemaker might be interested in what we have to say, since many of the principles are also employed in the discipleship process for the female-to-female model. Wives may be intrigued as well to read and discover more about the process involving her spouse and his Paul.

We give Biblical references for the various discipleship topics in the hope that you will examine the Word while reading this book, doing as the Berean Jews, who *searched the Scriptures every day to see if what Paul said was true*" (Acts 17:11). It is our heartfelt desire that what is written will glorify the Lord Jesus, His Word, and illuminate the process by which He takes over a life and lives His life through that man.

Each chapter listed in the **Table of Contents** covers a **different** topic and the topics are divided into four parts:

**Part I:** *"Discipleship Environment"* looks at culture, history, philosophy, etc. that set the process apart from typical religious activities.

**Part II:** *"Discipleship Process"* examines the basics of the disciple's walk. These basics include prayer, training, sending, etc., and are essential for the development of a spiritually mature man.

**Part III:** *"Character Development"* analyzes how a follower of Christ is transformed by the power of the Holy Spirit and Christ in him as he identifies his purpose, deals with truth, fear, etc.

**Part IV:** *"Aspects of the Disciple's Life"* looks at the issues he must deal with to successfully navigate the difficulties and challenges in today's world, such as family, work, stewardship, etc.

It's not necessary to read this book front to back. Look at *the Table of Contents* for a topic that catches your eye, read it and that might lead you to read other specific chapters. Starting by reading the foundational topics at the beginning of the book will be helpful, but certainly is not mandatory. Reading any of the chapters that interest you should be beneficial.

A chapter begins with a foundational Scripture, setting the tone for the topic. Biblical references are out of the New International Version (NIV) unless otherwise noted. These Scriptures make for excellent memory verses.

The next portion of the chapter is ***Paul's perspective.*** It's here that the modern day Paul shares from his personal philosophy on the various topics. What Paul is sharing is not theology, but what he has learned over many years of meeting with many men in the JPT process.

The third section is ***Timothy's story.*** It is here that a story is told about how this chapter's topic has impacted a Timothy's life as a result of the one-on-one discipleship process.

***Scripture references*** make up the next section. These will be useful for those who like to follow the Berean example and search the Scriptures to see for themselves what God's Word has to say about the topic. If you are leading another person or a group through the study of this topic, a review of these Scriptures before the meeting should be helpful as you lead them.

The chapter ends with ***Questions for reflection or discussion.*** ("Thoughts disentangle themselves as they cross over the lips and through the fingertips" – *Dawson Trotman, founder of The Navigators.)* If you are reading alone, you may want to write down your answers. If you are reading with someone else, you can meet and share your answers. When meeting with a group, the discussion of your answers should stimulate your minds to a greater in-depth examination of the topics. The chapters are short and not intended to cover the topics completely. Many fine books and study guides are available to those wishing to go deeper into a particular topic.

In conclusion, this book is intended as a reference source on how the Jesus, Paul, Timothy (JPT) relationship might view a topic in modern-day context. Therefore, we urge you to keep this book with your spiritual materials, such as your Bible, journals, study books, etc. so you can refer to it when a topic discussed in the book comes up with those you are discipling.

*-- Jay and Dave*

# Part I:

## *The Discipleship Environment*

# 1.
# Discipleship Philosophy

......................................................................

*"Therefore go and make disciples of all nations, baptizing them in the name of the Father and of the Son and of the Holy Spirit, and teaching them to obey everything I have commanded you. And surely I am with you always, to the very end of the age."*
*Matthew 28:19-20*

## Paul's perspective

Jesus' last words to His followers before He ascended into heaven to be with His Father are known as the Great Commission. He commissions me to go into the world and make disciples, teaching them to obey the commandments He has given to us. He promises not to leave me and I trust Him to provide for my needs if I obey His command to go and make disciples. *Discipleship is my calling.*

My philosophy of discipleship governs my values and behavior within the discipleship process. To clarify, I list below my philosophy of the discipleship process:

1. My mission is to impart to another the life of Jesus Christ that indwells me.
2. My method is one-on-one, life-on-life relationships.
3. My foundational truth is the Word of God.
4. My process is the application of the Word of God to our lives.
5. My goal is spiritual reproduction and multiplication of the life of Christ to the next generation and beyond. (See Appendix V for more detail on this process.)

This philosophy keeps me on point and helps me stay focused. To do this I need to be a man of spiritual integrity. In addition, Jesus instructs me to "seek Him first." My goal is for Christ to have a place of preeminence in me. In other words, Christ has first place in all things. Finally, I do not impose my philosophy on Timothy or others, because it is for me and my personal benefit. If God is to call men to be His disciple it must be His work, not mine.

What is a disciple? I like the way Dr. Howard Hendricks answers this question: "A disciple is a person who is in the process of becoming a man of God. And a man of God is a person who is in the process of becoming like Jesus."

This work of disciplemaking is offensive to Satan. It is spiritual warfare and without Jesus we are without the power needed to survive Satan's attacks that *WILL* come upon us. This means that discipleship is a war where God battles Satan for the souls, hearts and minds of people. Discipleship involves spiritual warfare and we will be under attack in the process. I am a soldier who must be clear about his mission, method, truth, assignment and goal. As soldiers in the service of our Lord, we must prepare ourselves. This means seeking Jesus first and being open and willing to having our character modified to resemble the character of Christ. We must be loyal to Jesus our commander and His leadership.

For me the battle became clear from day one, the day I accepted Christ. The old man in me wanted to steer me away from God, His decrees and His laws. Overcoming forty years of listening to Satan's directions has been an ongoing battle. But once I became a disciple of Christ, I began to win the battles and experience victory in God's battle with Satan for my mind, will, emotions, character and loyalty.

I don't like the idea of war. It sounds painful, a place where I could get hurt, even killed. My family might suffer as a result of my involvement. So why do I get involved in this battle? First, Jesus commanded me to go and make disciples. Second, I benefit from the process, as a Paul, even more than Timothy. The process is my life, it defines me, it compels me, it grows me and it feeds me. The discipleship process for me – it's a way of life.

## Timothy's story

More than thirty years ago I went through a painful divorce. I was a lost soul and my support group consisted of a few other lost men who attempted to comfort and entertain me. I medicated myself with women and substance abuse. This was a gut-wrenching, dark time for me. I handled the divorce improperly, creating an adversarial relationship with my ex-wife. One thing I never wanted was for my children to suffer the pain of a failed marriage.

But years later I met with my daughter and she said, "I am done. My marriage is over." The pain of my divorce resurfaced in a powerful way. Over the next months my second wife and I would walk through the acceptance of a family torn apart by my daughter's divorce. But this time it was different from 30 years ago. This time I had a wise, mature support group to support me as I became engaged in the spiritual warfare of Satan tearing a family apart.

For the past 10-plus years, my wife and I have teamed with three other like-minded couples as a core leadership group committed to the philosophy of one-on-one discipleship. During this time we shared the usual good and painful experiences common to the aging process of life. We have been a source of fellowship and encouragement to each other as we co-labored in the battle for men's souls.

A couple of years ago Satan turned his attack on our adult children. A nervous breakdown, two divorces and several encounters with the law have taken place in the children's lives. These kinds of events are emotionally very painful for parents and can be distractions from our ministries to those outside our genetic family.

We have shared the Gospel with our children and brought them up with the Word and around Christian fellowship. My Paul calls them "house-trained Christians," knowing the proper behaviors and being able to speak the Christian jargon. But God does not have any grandchildren. To put it another way, each child must be born again and live out his or her own personal relationship with the Lord. Our children cannot leverage their parents' relationship with God. They have to take care of their own business with Him, develop their own relationship with Jesus, and live out their own service for Him.

Our four-couple team has continued to fight a good fight, as good solders should, through the incredibly stressful events of the last two years, both personally and professionally. At times, our ministries seemed to be the only thing that made any sense. God promises He will work all things out for the good of those who love him and are called according to his purpose (Romans 8:28). In times that make little sense, it's the joy, gladness, rest and hope only He can provide that keeps us going in the battle to **go and make disciples.**

## Scripture references

Matthew 28:19-20; 2 Timothy 2:3-4; Matthew 6:33; Titus 1:5-9; 2 Timothy 4:7; Romans 8:28; Galatians 5:22-23

. . . . . . . . . . . . . . . . . . . . . . . . . . . . . . . . . . . . . . . . . . . . . . . . . . . . . . . . . . . .

## *Questions for reflection or discussion*

. . . . . . . . . . . . . . . . . . . . . . . . . . . . . . . . . . . . . . . . . . . . . . . . . . . . . . . . . . . .

What are your comments on this chapter?

What has been your personal experience with this topic?

Any Scriptures or principles discussed in this chapter you need to apply in your life?

# 2.
# The Calling

......................................

*"To them God has chosen to make known among the Gentiles
the glorious riches of this mystery, which is Christ in you, the
hope of glory. We proclaim him, admonishing and teaching
everyone with all wisdom, so that we may present everyone
perfect in Christ. To this end I labor, struggling with all
his energy, which so powerfully works in me."*
Colossians 1:27-29

## *Paul's perspective*

I have determined that my calling is to know Christ and to make
Him known to others. I have chosen to impart to others what I know of
Christ in hopes they will come to know him as I do and be faithful to
make Him known to others. It is for this cause that I invest time in men
that I trust will become layman witnesses and a Paul to others. It is my
hope these laymen will in turn adapt to their culture and reach the next
generation where they live for Christ.

Generational spiritual multiplication is the way one-on-one discipleship reproduces itself and builds a remnant of next-generation followers
of Christ, as we wait on the Lord's Day, the day of His return.

The apostle Paul's calling, using all his energy, was to proclaim Christ
to everyone, teaching them so they could become perfect in Christ as he
himself strived to be. Paul explains how he goes about accomplishing his
calling in that he trusted Timothy to teach other reliable men with the
things Paul had taught him. It is through this man-to-man process that
the next generations of disciples are born and become mature.

In this example, Paul is the first generation and Timothy is the second generation. Paul and Timothy each disciple a man, thus we have
four disciples. In the subsequent generations we have eight, then sixteen,

then thirty-two and so on. When the fourth generation begins to reproduce we can see God is using us to make His disciples and build a movement of people committed to disciplemaking.

During the initial years, an evangelist – by addition – may surpass the
disciplemaker in the number of those who become a follower of Jesus.
For example, if the evangelist has one new follower a day he would have
365 at the end of year one, whereas the disciplemaker would only have
one. If we follow the process for 32 years, however, we see an incredible, indisputable difference. Over that time period, evangelistic addition
would yield 11,680 new followers, and that is good, without question.
But multiplication would yield 4,294,967,296 new followers and future
disciplemakers – more than four billion! As they say, you do the math.

Multiplication of the faithful is God's plan and His calling to those
who are followers. Multiplication is a more effective process long-term
than addition. Rather than just adding new believers, each new believer
becomes a reproducer. Thus, each reproducer sees his faith in Christ
reproduced in many others who also do the same. This process exponentially surpasses addition with each proceeding generation.

This process creates opportunities to develop a team of disciplemakers who become part of my spiritual family. It is in this family I am able
to experience the relationships by which the fullness of our life in Christ
reveals itself. In this environment, people learn about and experience the
callings of salvation, evangelism, spiritual rest, and discipleship. Jesus
calls us to rest; He tells us that if we come to Him, He will give us rest for
our souls.

As Jesus led, we are called to lead both our genetic and spiritual
families, helping them become disciples and disciplemakers. Jesus com-
missioned His followers to evangelize and to go and make disciples,
teaching them to obey everything He had commanded them. A person's
calling to one-on-one discipleship is a very effective way of participating in the Great Commission we have been given by our Lord. Jesus
also calls men to salvation, as illustrated in His speaking to Nicodemus
about being born again.

As I have discipled men over a long period of my life, many of these
men are younger than me and will continue the process after I go to the
grave. Since this process continues after I go to heaven, this validates
the prophet Isaiah's statement that *"a small one can become a thousand"*

(Isaiah 60:22). The Lord will use this person to enlarge the Kingdom. A faithful person can become a thousand through the multiplication process of one-on-one discipleship that continues after he dies.

Not all followers are willing to be discipled in a one-on-one setting, and therefore are not able to teach others in this way. Because the discipleship ministry is *caught* from a Paul, not *taught* in a classroom setting, it's important to observe it and experience it with our own Paul. If a person submits to personal discipleship, then he may determine that he is called to this type of personal ministry.

## Timothy's story

The first man I attempted to disciple was a man who was close to me. Because of my immaturity, we got into an argument over the deity of Christ. He proved not to be a teachable man, at least with me.

The second man was younger than me and was drawn to me because we both were in the same sales profession. During the time we were meeting in a discipling relationship, this man invited Christ into his life and then discipled another man who did the same. Both of these men have shared the Gospel with their families and many others.

Over the years there have been others. Each man has been a unique learning experience for me. Not all of them have gone on to become disciplemakers, but each man has blessed me with a relationship centered on the Lord Jesus. These men are a part of my spiritual family and we co-labor each in our own ways for the cause of the Gospel. Relationships like these are rich, beyond words of explanation.

## Scripture references

Colossians 1:27-29; 2 Timothy 2:2; Isaiah 60:22; Matthew 28:19-20

## *Questions for reflection or discussion*

What are your comments on this chapter?

What has been your personal experience with this topic?

Any Scriptures or principles discussed in this chapter you need to apply in your life?

# 3.
# Culture

·····················

*"Dear friends, I urge you, as aliens and strangers in the world,*
*to abstain from sinful desires, which war against your soul."*
1 Peter 2:11

## Paul's perspective

I find myself uncomfortable with the culture that we are living in today. Liberals and conservatives whack away at each other 24/7 on TV, in print and over the Internet. I am challenged to be tolerant with: multiculturalism, relativism, downward mobility, redefining the family, and technology that fills my time. Advertising promotes the pursuit of self-fulfillment, and the culture is filled with personal and socially destructive behavior.

Some experts call these times the Post-Christian Age or the end of the Judeo-Christian Culture. Another term I see used to describe this period is Post-Modernity. Dogmatic religion no longer prevails, and the secular man I live and work around is often a blank page when it comes to spirituality.

Religion is preached from afar over the airwaves or from podiums, often by those who promise prosperity and are amassing personal wealth from their ministries. We live in a drug culture where both legal and illegal drugs are used to medicate the emotional pain life brings. Sin is not called sin; instead, it is identified and justified as dysfunction for the sake of political correctness.

In this culture, the philosophy of relativism promotes every man deciding his own truth based on what is good for him. The web site *all-aboutphilosophy.org* defines Cultural Relativism as the view that moral or ethical systems, which vary from culture to culture, are all equally valid and no one system is really "better" than any other. This is based on the idea that there is no ultimate standard of good or evil, so every judgment about right and wrong is a product of society. Therefore, any opinion on morality or ethics is subject to the cultural perspective of each person. Ultimately, this means that no moral or ethical system can be considered the "best," or "worst," and no particular moral or ethical position can actually be considered "right" or "wrong." In conclusion, absolute truth is not a reality because truth is now defined as relative, depending on the beliefs of the person who defines it.

The apostle Paul wrote to the church in Corinth, made up mostly of Gentiles, concerning how to live for Christ in a corrupt culture. Corinth was a major metropolis, the most important city in Achaia, where one would encounter philosophies encouraging each man to create his own truth. The apostle Paul did not need to deal with the distractions of technology. Most communication came written by hand or spoken face-to-face. Paul encouraged a person-to-person relational witness of the indwelling power of Christ in the follower's life. In a face-to-face relationship, one can see the truth of Jesus lived out in another person, as the Corinthians had seen it exhibited in Paul's life when he lived with them.

One thing that will hinder a Paul's ministry is getting caught up in partisan opinion concerning the political environment of this age. God has placed certain public officials in office for reasons that make little sense to me. The principles I must remember are as follows: to honor all men, love the brotherhood, fear God, and honor those in authority.

Leadership bashing is a popular habit among many in our country, along with the anger and fear it exhibits. Our culture has become driven by anger about the past, and fear of the future. Elections seem to swing on one, the other, or both. Because of this pervasive fear and anger, public officials are not honored, let alone prayed for as instructed in Scripture.

Paul must do the right thing and fear God, not men. By honoring those in leadership, he is not only doing the right thing, but this also will open up his ministry to men on both sides of the political dilemmas facing our country. I think it is important to vote my convictions, but I am careful to keep them mostly to myself for the purposes of my ministry to all types of men.

Although Jesus was entrenched in an extremely political culture, he apparently took no position in it. Instead He involved Himself only in

His Father's business: *people.* In today's culture, I am challenged to stay focused on the call to make disciples of *all* men, and not be drawn into debating political, religious, or other differences. For me, the need to be opinionated or "right" about such matters is not an option. Such matters build up walls between me and the very people with whom I desire to build a relationship.

Younger people today are very relational, but in a different sense because they use technology – texting, for example – to communicate. By meeting face-to-face with them, they can learn from me about a new dimension of friendship. Having lunch, playing golf, tennis, or bringing them into my home are just a few ways to open the door into a man's life.

Older people today are more isolated at home and in business. They are glued to computers at work. When returning home they drive into the garage, hit the remote and emerge the next day only to return to their office computer. Their neighbors see them only when they put out the garbage. In Biblical times, people walked the streets and hung out at the public gates where they got to know their neighbors. Today, many people would be hard pressed to call most of their neighbors by name. Inviting others into my home is my primary strategy for reaching the isolated people of this culture.

As a businessman, I am forced to deal with cell phones, computers, the Internet, email and text messaging. These are some of today's cultural distractions that pose challenges when building relationships with those I hope to disciple. To be effective with those in today's culture, it's best to keep my focus on intimacy with Jesus and the mission of making disciples. One-on-one personal discipleship works in today's cultures, just as it worked in Corinth, because the nature of sinful man and the consequences of his sin have not changed. Also, God created us for relationships. To grow and mature in his faith, a man needs to meet Christ personally in the life of another living for Christ, such as a Paul. Opening our lives and our homes to a man, a couple, or even a family, is the best way to establish relationships that lead to evangelism and discipleship.

### Timothy's story

I spent the first 30 years of my life immersed in the secular culture. I was living and competing using the rules of the secular culture. This relativistic approach to life would self-destruct because much of what I lived and believed just was not grounded in absolute truth.

I first met my Paul on the tennis court, as we competed in a tennis league. We enjoyed many spirited, competitive matches as partners and opponents. He was 20 years ahead of me in both age and tennis experience, and we became partners. Once the tennis game was over we usually ended up sitting around, talking about all kinds of things. As a result, we connected and became friends.

For several years he would invite me and my wife into his home for a Christmas party hosted for a number of their friends. The party was typical at first, with food and drink, conversation, and then he would call everyone together and read the Christmas story, a most enjoyable moment. Usually I would stay after the others had left, just to get a little closer to my new friend.

As friends, we surely appeared as an unsuitable match for each other. Most people looked at him as a righteous, mature guy in control of his life, while I came across on the tennis court as an out-of-control, immature guy with a filthy mouth. But he hung with me despite the obvious differences in our character and behavior.

His teenage son was into drugs and experiencing loads of trouble. I quizzed him as to how a Christian man could have such a son. He explained to me how this results from our children's free will choices. What impacted me was his unconditional love and acceptance of his son.

When I began to meet with my Paul in the study of the Bible, things began to change. For about a year, we used a study called *Operation Timothy* that looked at the Biblical basics, such as the Bible's credibility, Jesus' identity, the definition of sin, and God's forgiveness. Looking at the Word, I discovered the logic of God many times was the opposite of the culture's logic. It has often been difficult for me to give up my worldly logic. Making the same mistakes over and over is painful, yet often necessary in order for me to learn to die to self and live God's way.

One night I called my Paul, informing him I was ready to invite Jesus into my life and follow Christ. He suggested we talk about it the next morning over coffee. But I could not wait, so I asked Jesus into my life that night. We rejoiced the next morning over my decision. I am thankful for my Paul's patience with me.

Soon afterward, we began to go deeper into the Word together. Although Scripture memory was difficult for me, once I began taking the Word in to my mind and heart, I began changing. It became evident, to me and my Paul, I was an authentic follower of Christ. This whole process took about seven years from the time we first met on the tennis court. Over this period I was in his home many times and we got to know each other's wives and children.

Whether it is sports, politics, or business, I have always enjoyed being correct. Dying to my need to be right is a major, ongoing challenge, but with my Paul's modeling, I am gradually beginning to be less consumed in this area. This new attitude is paying dividends as more people are drawn to me. Thus, they become friends and when the time is right, I can begin sharing Christ with them.

## Scripture references

1 Peter 2:11; 1 Peter 2:13-17; 1 Corinthians 9:19-22; Matthew 28:19-20; 1 Corinthians 10:24: 1 John 2:15-16; Romans 12:2

........................................................................................

## Questions for reflection or discussion

........................................................................................

What are your comments on this chapter?


What has been your personal experience with this topic?


Are there any Scriptures or principles discussed in this chapter you need to apply in your life?

# 4.
# Secular Man

....................................

*"For this reason we also thank God without ceasing, because
when you received the word of God which you heard from us,
you welcomed it not as the word of men, but as it is in truth, the
word of God, which also effectively works in you who believe."*
1 Thessalonians 2:13 (NKJV)

## Paul's perspective

The process of winning and discipling secular men who will become
Timothys takes place in a world that is undergoing constant change.
Today's culture differs from 30-plus years ago in that many people grow
up today without the influences of the Judeo-Christian environment that
influenced previous generations in this country. At one time, America
was primarily a country of Christian values and morals. Understanding
the secular culture and its influence on men that we hope to reach for
Christ is helpful.

The secular education system, entertainment world and news media
have imposed a new value system on the current generations, particularly
those under the age of sixty. Truth is no longer presented as absolute, but
as relative. This philosophy is called relativism and revolves around the
notion that every man is free to determine his own truths based on what
he believes to be in his best interest. Relativism leads people down paths
not based on absolute truth, resulting in eventual failure. They must then
start over, traveling a different path that now looks good to them. A rela-
tivist is stuck in a cycle of start, failure and restart.

Timothy and I live in an increasingly secular culture, yet it is not
unlike the secular culture Jesus and the apostle Paul encountered in the
first century before the spread of Christianity. In reaching the men of

their time – their disciples – with the truth of God's Word, they presented us with an example to follow.

The apostle Paul describes himself as a free man belonging to no one, able to befriend the religious Jews and the secular Greeks, those under the law and those not having the law. He becomes all things to all men so that by all possible means he might see some saved. Paul is a servant to all men for the cause of winning and discipling both the secular and religious lost. He meets with people in their city, home and culture. The religious establishment pressures him to place those that were converted under the legalism of the Jewish religious establishment, but Paul continues to teach the freedom of a relationship with Christ. He writes in Romans 8:1 that there is no condemnation for those who are in Christ Jesus. Because of Paul's example, the movement of the Gentiles becoming followers of Christ spreads exponentially throughout the world's secular cultures for the next 400 years.

As our culture grows more secular, more opportunities to disciple the secular person become available. Building a friendship with them and avoiding being stereotyped as a "religious person" with an institutional agenda is the best way to get them to look at the Bible as a source of reliable truth.

On the other end of the spectrum is the religious man who, because he has spent considerable time in the institutional religious system, will have traditions and the mindset of that religion. His challenge is to set aside what was imparted to him through this group in favor of engaging in one-on-one discipleship. The institution's group and assembly teaching approach may not allow for the increased degree of transparency and accountability found in the one-on-one discipleship process. My method with the religious man is the same: pray for him, and cultivate and sow the Word into the field – his mind. Both types of people are equally challenging to disciple and distinctive in their struggles of allowing Christ to be the Lord of their lives.

Secular people present a unique challenge, in that building a relationship with them takes considerable time. It involves looking at the Scriptures together as the source of truth. Because secular people have little, if any, solid religious background or experience, they come to us as a Biblical blank page. Watching them discover the truth of God's Word is an exciting and rewarding experience. The mind of the secular man is depraved and skeptical to the extent that his values and belief system are being challenged; coming to embrace Christ involves rejection of many of his former opinions and thought patterns.

When the Word of God hits his mind, little by little it begins impacting him. This is an ongoing battle, and usually a slow one. Therefore it requires that Paul display plenty of patience and an unwavering commitment to stick with him throughout the entire process. In the beginning it's similar to spoon-feeding food to a baby. I begin by praying that God would open up his secular mind to the Word. Ted DeMoss, former president of CBMC, often made the statement, "How dare we speak to men about God before we speak to God about men."

A man's mind represents the field being worked. I try my hardest to cultivate this field and prepare it for the sowing of the seed, the Word of God. The seed is sown over and over, watered, and with time it takes root and transforms the secular man's mind into one that readily receives the truth of Christ. This truth changes him into a new creation, a work of God.

Jesus helps us understand the field, the heart and mind of a man, in Matthew 13:18-23: *"Listen then to what the parable of the sower means: When anyone hears the message about the Kingdom and does not understand it, the evil one comes and snatches away what was sown in his heart. This is the seed sown along the path. The one who received the seed that fell on rocky places is the man who hears the word and at once receives it with joy. But since he has no root, he lasts only a short time. When trouble or persecution comes because of the word, he quickly falls away. The one who received the seed that fell among the thorns is the man who hears the word, but the worries of this life and the deceitfulness of wealth choke it, making it unfruitful. But the one who received the seed that fell on good soil is the man who hears the word and understands it. He produces a crop, yielding a hundred, sixty or thirty times what was sown."*

The renewing of the secular man's mind is a very long process, sometimes taking eight to ten years or even longer to take root and grow. Establishing a relationship with him so we can sow the Word into him is our work. In the beginning the ground – his mind – is hard. Through our relationship, the ground softens, receiving water and fertilizer so the seed takes root and begins to produce little plants. These plants grow into a field of God's righteousness in the man's mind. As a Paul, I have the privilege of planting the seeds and watching them grow.

*Note: see Appendix V for a summary outline of this process.*

## Timothy's story

A Timothy of mine and I have put together a "businessman's luncheon" in a professional environment. This is not a Bible study, but a secular lunch meeting with an unspoken spiritual agenda. These gatherings are an attempt to lead secular men to the Scriptures by meeting every other week in a room where the men who come can eat lunch and talk, or just listen. The idea is that the secular men will get to hear about and see our lives in a non-threatening way. As we eat lunch, topics of interest to men such as money, needs, margin, success, boundaries, rest and others are discussed in a non-religious, non-teaching environment. It was during one of these lunches that I met my Timothy.

This future Timothy was a secular man that began showing up at our luncheons. He sat in the group for a year and a half. At one particular breakfast downtown, a guest from Atlanta spoke that had a background similar to Timothy's, one with which he could relate. This speaker shared his life, his failures, his fears, and how eventually Jesus Christ came into his life. At the end of the meeting, Timothy said to me, "I have never heard anything like that in my life." I invited him to meet with me the next week and start talking about the subjects the speaker had raised. We began having lunch every couple of weeks over the next year; little by little we discussed, talked and looked at some materials. What troubled him most were the changes, as he had no absolute truth on which he could bank. His dad was a secular Jewish man and his mom had some religious roots, but he had not been involved in church in any way. So this was a whole new experience – and understandably fearful for him.

One day I gave him an excerpt from *The Message Bible*, written by Eugene Peterson. My Timothy was unaware what I gave him was from a Bible, because this version is written using the language of today's culture. He came back to me and said, "I really like that story you gave me. I would like to read some more of it." So I gave him the Whole New Testament *Message Bible*, because I just happened to have a copy in my car. He began to read and, little by little, God began getting a hold of his heart. I did not try to bring him into the Kingdom because I was trusting God would do that when he was ready.

One day he came to me and told me a story of a friend who had just been sent to prison. Timothy and his sister had gone to the trial. After sitting through the murder trial, he believed the man was innocent, but he was found guilty. After the trial he sat in his car for a couple of hours outside a convenience store and sorted through why God would want an innocent man to go to prison. In the hours he sat in his car, God began to show him he needed Jesus Christ in his life.

The next time we met, he told me about how he had received Jesus Christ. Not long before this he and his wife had been willing to come to a week-long vacation week retreat because he was being drawn into the Kingdom. At the end of this week in our small group, he said he was like a guy walking around the swimming pool but had not yet jumped in. The week left a lasting impact on him because he discovered the people at the retreat were so different. They accepted him where he was, and did not even ask him to change his ways – or to jump into the pool.

This is the story of a totally secular guy coming to Christ. Over a four-year period, one stepping stone at a time, he moved through the process by being involved with his Paul and other men in the movement, and God brought the harvest of his soul in His own timing.

## Scripture references

1 Thessalonians 2:13 (KJV); Matthew 13:18-23; 1 Corinthians 9:19-22; Romans 8:1

......................................................................

# Questions for reflection or discussion

......................................................................

What are your comments on this chapter?


What has been your personal experience with this topic?


Any Scriptures or principles discussed in this chapter you need to apply in your life?

# 5.
# Layman Environment

· · · · · · · · · · · · · · · · · · · · · · · · · · · · · · · · · · · · · · · · · · · · · · · · · · · · · · ·

*"For where two or three come together*
*in my name, there am I with them."*
*Matthew 18:20*

## Paul's perspective

Throughout the book of Genesis we observe that the primary men God spoke to and those that carried out His plans for the Jewish race were laymen. Men such as Adam, Noah, Abraham and his male descendents were not full-time religious workers, but laymen, people with ordinary jobs.

In the first four books of the New Testament, Jesus' disciples are identified as laymen. Several are fishermen, such as Peter, and Matthew was a tax collector. Luke, the writer of the books of Luke and Acts, was a physician. Jesus did not conduct his ministry with the disciples in the Temple in a classroom setting. He took them out into the world, often away from town, to places where they could be alone and He could disciple them, many times one-on-one.

The apostle Paul's occupation is described as a layman tentmaker, which means frequently he had to fund his ministry with a job as he traveled from city to city. The people he stayed with in the various cities were the ones he focused on primarily. These laymen were the people he counted on to win over and disciple their colleagues, friends and acquaintances. Once he had discipled these key laymen, who would repeat this process, he then moved on.

In a poll I read about, businessmen were asked who they would feel the most comfortable with in discussing spiritual matters – a pastor, a missionary, or another businessman. The overwhelming majority said they would choose another businessman. Businessmen are comfortable meeting with other businessmen about the intimate details of their life. It's not that they devalue the pastor or dislike him; perhaps they think the pastor has trouble relating to where they live and work. The layman is in a great position to get alongside the secular man where he lives, works, and spends his leisure time. It's in the marketplace where the layman/businessman can come alongside another man and carry out the cultivation and sowing process of lifestyle evangelism that eventually leads to one-on-one discipleship.

My perspective of the layman environment Timothy and I live in is that most believers are church people. They are committed to their local church as the place where they exercise their faith most effectively. It is a place where people feel at home with others they think are spiritually like-minded.

The majority of these churched laymen are more passive than pro-active in the affairs of the local church. Many lead compartmentalized lives that separate their religion, business, and personal lives. The engaged church laymen are involved in roles of giving, teaching, works of service, administration, etc. However, the typical layman often sees the ministry in terms of meetings he attends, much like his work-related meetings. After a while, since he is not getting paid, he becomes less and less fulfilled, losing interest in the meetings that don't lend themselves to intimacy.

This is not an anti-church theme, but the fact is that the local church is seldom fruitfully involved in one-on-one discipleship. It effectively teaches in large and small groups much like the public and private education systems. In reality, however, many students want and need personal attention beyond what the normal educational system provides. Consequently, circumstances lead them to find a tutor or friend outside the education system, someone they can personally identify with that will help them get the desired one-on-one attention they need.

In a similar sense, one-on-one discipleship is most effective when done outside the confines and boundaries of a local religious or denominational organization. With Timothy, I concentrate on the basics of our relationship with Jesus and let him see how I relate to Jesus daily. I see our relationship as separate from Timothy's involvement in a religion or a belief system that he may have come from or is now embracing.

Being a layman, I support my ministry from proceeds generated through my business. Some men who do this kind of ministry have been called to be full-time, vocational Christian workers. They perform certain tasks for Christian organizations that pay them. They also do one-on-one discipleship much the same as I do, while they support themselves through compensation that their Christian organization job provides. In truth, however, we all are full-time workers, just compensated differently. Look at it this way: there is no such thing as a part-time Christian, and all Christians are called to serve God and His people. So in reality, we *all* are called to "full-time Christian service."

The marketplace is the perfect environment for the layman to effectively win the hearts of secular businessmen, earn the right to speak into their lives, and eventually to disciple them. Having an effective tool to use for discipling another man is critical for a layman worker. The layman worker usually doesn't have the time or training to prepare special materials and lessons necessary to train Timothy. For that reason, such a discipleship tool has been developed, and used by the movement for many years: It's called *Operation Timothy (OT)*.

(Note: *Operation Timothy* books are available through www.CBMC.com.)

## *Timothy's story*

Bob joined one of the company's business units about two years ago. When he secured a piece of the enterprise and that business was open to ecommerce (my area of expertise), he subsequently included me in the sales calls to support that activity. Bob and I would drive to the Southwest part of Houston, which gave us 30-40 minutes of "windshield" time. Spending time with Bob, I began to hear about some of the pain and discomfort in his life. Inevitably, these conversations gave rise to a meaningful spiritual discussion.

I learned Bob had been reared in a Godly home. His parents loved the Lord and encouraged him to do likewise. Bob admitted, as he gave me a version of his spiritual journey, that he had turned his back on God and done many things he was sincerely ashamed of. In turn, I shared my story with him, which gave him license to become even more transparent. We sat and discussed over lunch how patient God had been with both of us. We ended the time with a brief prayer.

About a week later I felt the urging of the Spirit to call Bob and ask him if he would like to do an investigative Bible study with me. I promised the study would result in a deeper relationship with Jesus and a greater ability to understand and apply God's Word. He seemed genuinely excited by the chance to meet and explore *Operation Timothy (OT)*. We have been meeting for about four months, and are now past the midpoint of Book Two in the study. Bob is eager to do the memory work, and I am equally eager to share how I have learned that the Lord uses the memory verses to enhance our lives and our impact on others.

Bob tells me that although he attends church, leads a "care-group," and has a wife who seeks the Lord, our weekly meetings in *OT* are by far his most rewarding time. "I get my life from these meetings," says Bob. Although I travel quite a bit, Bob sees me making the meetings a priority. I want him to know this because I have assured him Satan would mount all of Hell against us to ensure we don't meet. "Not on my watch," I say!

What a privilege it is to witness God reclaiming one of His saints and maturing the man before my very eyes. I am resigned to the fact that I have nothing to contribute, that it is the Savior who must be front and center in our meetings. I merely have to show up and be available. What a delight it is to simply participate and to be in the game. Thank you, Jesus!

## Scripture references
Matthew 18:20; Matthew 4:19; Acts 18:3

..................................................................

## Questions for reflection or discussion

..................................................................

What are your comments on this chapter?

What has been your personal experience with this topic?

Any Scriptures or principles discussed in this chapter you need to apply in your life?

# 6.
# History

## Paul's perspective

Beginning with Jesus' example with His followers, and then with the apostle Paul and those he invested in, we observe that personal time with the Lord is critical for the believer to experience transformation through the indwelling Holy Spirit, which is brought into the life of the follower of Christ. Jesus and His Spirit have indwelled His followers for more than 2,000 years. History encourages me and I am confident that if I invest in men, as did those who came before me, I will lay the foundation for a process that will continue long after I am gone. The results can be that a person such as me can reproduce a thousand others (as the verse above states) because once started, spiritual multiplication continues far beyond our physical death.

There was a point in my life when I became interested in genealogy. I felt a need to know more about my family's history. So I asked those in my family who were a little older than me what they knew or had heard about our history. It turned out that I am the descendant of some very ordinary people who lived very ordinary lives, nothing special to report. But my spiritual genealogy is loaded with men who lived extraordinary, fruitful and exciting lives in their commitment to the Lord. My genetic family was given to me, and I had no choice in the matter. My spiritual family is one I have chosen to claim as my spiritual lineage because of our common commitment to one-on-one discipleship

In the New Testament, the discipleship process I know is modeled after Jesus' one-on-one time with the disciples and Paul's one-on-one time with Timothy (and others). When I read the four Gospels – Matthew, Mark, Luke, and John – I see the original twelve disciples were discipled by Jesus. Being God with man, He demonstrated the life of God in His personal time with the disciples. Paul personally met Jesus on the road to Damascus and his life was forever changed. Prior to encountering Jesus, Paul had been trained as a Pharisee by Rabbi Gamaliel. He genuinely believed the followers of Christ were a grievous threat to the Jewish religion. As a result of his encounter with Jesus on the road to Damascus, however, Paul became a follower and was then discipled by Barnabas over a period of years.

Timothy was one of Paul's disciples and his letters, 1 Timothy and 2 Timothy, further describe their relationship. Timothy is described as a faithful, teachable man qualified to teach others the things he had learned from Paul.

The modern-day model emerged more than 70 years ago before World War II in The Navigators' ministry, led by a man named Dawson Trotman. "Daws," as he was called, defined the process. The great evangelist Billy Graham recruited Daws to follow up with the people that had responded at his crusades and wanted someone to meet with them. One of the men who became involved in the crusade follow-up with Daws was Dan Piatt. Dan met and discipled a man named Pete George.

Men that Daws and The Navigators had discipled eventually served in World War II on ships, at training bases, and in combat zones. Pete George was one of these men. Pete eventually met Joe Coggeshall in Italy, playing pool at a military service center. They established a friendship and Pete discipled Joe. In my spiritual lineage, Pete is my great-grandfather and Joe is my grandfather. These men emerged from the war skilled as "Pauls" in the art of discipleship.

After World War II ended, many Navigators, also known as "Navs," took their ministries to colleges and began to win and disciple students there in the late 1940s and '50s. Navs also went into business and began to win and disciple businessmen. My spiritual grandfather, Joe, was one such man. He imparted the principles of discipleship to Dave, my spiritual father, who imparted them to me. Joe, Dave and I are products of the pre-1960s Judeo-Christian culture that pervaded America.

The men I am discipling one-on-one today are more and more products of the post-Judeo-Christian culture. Their Post-Modern philosophy rejects absolutes. These men bring a worldview to the process that is very contrary to the worldview that accompanied me into the Kingdom. With that understanding, I am making an effort to meet these men where they are. I am not compromising my worldview, but I am not imposing my view upon them. The Scriptures and the Holy Spirit must be their teachers with regard to the absolute truth. Jesus said in the Scriptures that He came into the world to testify to the truth, and everyone on the side of truth would listen to Him. I can only point men to Jesus, just as those who came before pointed me to Him.

History testifies that Jesus' work is valid and can be done in any culture, with all manner of men, because He and the Gospel are trans-cultural. Make no mistake – discipleship is God's work. I have only the privilege of walking alongside a man and observing God's work in that man. Jesus' work is done in His own way, in His own timing, as has been the case for all of history.

## Timothy's story

The process of being discipled by another man more spiritually mature than me was very appealing. In my late 30's, I became increasingly interested in spiritual matters. As a child, I experienced some organized religion, but in my teenage years my interest in religion ceased to exist.

As I began to seek spiritual direction later in life, I found the diversity of religious choices confusing. The idea of examining the Bible with another man, a businessman with whom I could relate, seemed to make sense. I reasoned that after I had a basic knowledge of the Scriptures, I could make an informed decision about religions or denominational choices. But as I examined the history of the Bible, it became increasingly clear that discipleship relationships served as Jesus' – and then Paul's – method for developing spiritual maturity. In one-on-one discipleship I discovered that Jesus came to establish a relationship with me, not to give me a religion to follow.

History is important to me. It validates truth and exposes man's struggles that result from decisions flawed by incorrect thinking. As I became a student of the Bible, I was amazed at how man's "truth" is often opposite from the truth of the Bible. I have heard it said this way: Religion is man's way to reach out to God. Jesus Christ and the Bible are

God's way to reach down to man. In other words, religion is man's idea about God. The Bible is God speaking to man about who He is.

The history of Christian religion has been one of change and confusion for more than 1,600 years. On the other hand, the Bible has remained the same over a much longer time period. History is partly the reason I made my choice to follow Jesus and obey the Bible's directive to go and make disciples.

### Scripture references

Isaiah 60:22; John 18:37b, John 1:1, 1:14; Acts 7:54-28:31; 2 Timothy 2:2; Matthew 28:19-20

. . . . . . . . . . . . . . . . . . . . . . . . . . . . . . . . . . . . . . . . . . . . . . . . . . . . . . . . . . . . .

## Questions for reflection or discussion

. . . . . . . . . . . . . . . . . . . . . . . . . . . . . . . . . . . . . . . . . . . . . . . . . . . . . . . . . . . . .

What are your comments on this chapter?

What has been your personal experience with this topic?

Any Scriptures or principles discussed in this chapter you need to apply in your life?

# 7.
# Plan
. . . . . . . . . . . .

*"My dear children, for whom I am again in the pains of
childbirth until Christ is formed in you."*
*Galatians 4:19*

### Paul's perspective

While discipling men, I have a plan and a desire to help them grow
and mature into effective followers of Christ. For this to take place, Christ
must become fully formed in their hearts. This spiritual maturity process
develops the same way growth occurs in our own family. Children grow
up and develop peer relationships, then move out and begin the process
of having their own families.

In the beginning, I will meet with Timothy as often as his need
requires, even a couple of times a week in the early days of the relationship. Walking with young believers often causes a lot of pain while they
are spiritually developing, much like a mother who suffers a lot of pain
in the formation of a child in her womb and its birth. The pain doesn't
stop when the birth occurs. A baby's growth steps can be painful for the
parent as the child learns to hold its bottle, goes through diaper training,
learns to walk and yield to parental discipline. Spiritual baby-stepping
can be similarly painful for Paul as Christ is being formed in Timothy.

As time goes on and Timothy grows spiritually from infancy in his
faith, his need to be with me decreases. My role throughout this process
is to serve this man by giving my life away to him. At times he may treat
me poorly, no better than a stray. However, no ingratitude should hinder
me from serving him.

As I walk side-by-side with Timothy, I team with him in various
events and ministry forms. I help him develop in the following areas:
realizing the purpose of his life; finding a vision for his ministry; learning

effective lifestyle evangelism; experiencing community building; finding men to disciple and discipling them; sending the process out to other locations; using ministry tools and events to reach others, and building teams.

How long does it take for a disciple to mature in the process? It truly differs with every man. God is the one orchestrating the length of our time together. I may only have a few days with a man, but that would be the exception. The quick-to-mature man may show great progress in two to three years. The average man begins catching on in five years, while some take ten or more. Leaders begin to show maturity in seven to ten years. This building of a mature Paul is a lifelong process involving my continued, patient walk with him, as well as other relationships and lifelong experiences orchestrated by God.

The critical part of this process is Timothy meeting with another man as a Paul in one-on-one discipleship. It has been said that you have not made a disciple until your disciple makes a disciple. Timothy must find a man to disciple, a man he can give a little piece of his heart to, if he is to successfully carry out the plan. It is important for me as his Paul to help him overcome whatever obstacles may be holding him back. Until this happens, the discipling I have done has not been successful as a process that is reproducing a disciplemaker. To complete the plan, this third generation removed from me must also find a man to disciple. This usually occurs between years three and ten. When this takes place, Timothy develops a need to be with men doing the same thing, meeting with men in one-on-one discipleship. In this group he will begin to cross-pollinate with other like-minded men.

The group consists of peers that are also Pauls, who hold one another accountable to encourage the healthy growth of each other as reproducers of reproductive followers of Christ. They talk through their struggles and are there for each other. The group will meet a couple of times a month to encourage one another in their walk with Christ and the discipling of a man. When Timothy begins to develop this other resource, he weans off of the fathering relationship with me as his primary or only source of encouragement. He now has peers, and this growth releases me to go on and begin the process again with another man.

Admittedly, this process of disciplining men most of the time will bring some degree of suffering and grief into the life of a Paul. Timothy's and my sufferings are shaping our character, resulting in our growth in Christ-likeness. God is expecting us to engage in this very important endeavor of walking with a man as his spiritual father. A Janis Joplin song lyric says to "take another little piece of my heart." This is what happens with Paul as each man takes a little piece of his heart. Sometimes he is tread upon, while other times it's a blessing. It's good to know that God orchestrates for His own purposes these experiences of the heart.

The plan of walking with a maturing man – and the pain it brings – will go on as he experiences the inevitable hardships of life. I have stood with them as they went through struggling marriages, some that ended in divorce; challenges in overcoming addictions; financial turmoil; serious illnesses; problems with difficult children; issues with in-laws; incarceration. Sadly, I have even had to endure the pain of seeing two men, in whom I had invested considerable time, energy and emotion, that still gave in to despair and committed suicide. There have been others that just chose to end our discipling relationship for various reasons.

Yet, these experiences are God's way of working in my life to deepen my relationship with Him. Each time He has affirmed that He's the one in control, that the responsibility is His. Mine is just to be faithful and available to opportunities He sends my way. God's desire is to have a meaningful relationship with us. It's often through pain that He achieves this end.

## Timothy's story

My story is about discipleship work with three different men. Each man is uniquely different and therefore has challenged me to ask for wisdom and understanding so I might effectively serve each of them. This story covers a period of 24-plus years and involves a plan I had in mind for each of these men to fully reach maturity in their relationship with Christ.

Timothy #1 came into my life because another man whom I discipled introduced us about ten years ago. He was in his late 20's, with a wife and three young children.  His wife was religious, but he had no spiritual background. The rituals and traditions of religion made no sense to him.

Using the *Operation Timothy* books as the discipleship tool, we dove into the Bible. Within about 90 days he invited Christ into his life as a repentant sinner. His strength as a disciple was his faithfulness to memorize Scriptures, and thus his worldview began to change rapidly as he absorbed the truths of God's Word.

His struggle had been with the lack of order in his life. Gradually, over the years he has ordered his finances, career and family life. He is a team player and gathers people with skill and ease. He has been involved with several men in the one-on-one discipleship process as a Paul.

Timothy #2 is about 15 years younger than me and we met about 25 years ago. We were both in real estate brokerage. He was a zealous spiritual person who had been proactive in various Christian endeavors. He was hungry for fellowship and faithful to get into the work, so we used the *Operation Timothy* books as a reason to meet together and cast the vision of one-on-one discipleship.

He struggled with his wife, who came from a very dysfunctional family. Her mother and sister lived close by, and the chaos these relationships created was used by God to humble him and grow character in both of us.

He attracts men from all cultures and has discipled a number of them. One man he discipled has gone on to disciple a number of other men. His teenage boys challenge him, and he has grown more and more attached to the spiritual family of the movement. Our friendship and involvement in business has been a wonderful blessing to me over the years. The humbling process we both have experienced has brought us into greater maturity with the formation of Christ-like character in our lives. I consider him an authentic friend that stands ready to help me in any way he is able.

Timothy #3 and I met over 20 years ago. We both had offices in the same part of town and got together because he was interested in the idea of being a witness in the marketplace and was open to being discipled. Though his parents divorced, his father had remained faithful to him and he exhibited this same caring personality that his father had.

His wife, who brought two young boys into the marriage, proved to be a source of conflict between them. He was building a successful law practice that often overwhelmed him. Through all of that, we built a solid friendship. He is a loyal, loving friend who has walked through many difficult circumstances with me.

Early on he got the idea of investing his life into other men. It took about ten years for God to provide him a man who proved to be a faithful, available, teachable Timothy. The man God brought to him was geographically convenient for him to meet with and this relationship blossomed. Then this Timothy's company transferred him to another city, making it about a three-hour drive away from each other. This did not deter either of them, however, and they continued the process, becoming more and more connected and committed to each other. The Timothy has now moved back to this city and has been discipling other men for several years.

This is a man that has blessed me in so many ways, and we co-labor as peers in the overseeing of the movement. He is about 15 years younger and my impact on him through Christ could continue for years after I am called home by my Heavenly Father.

These three Timothys are examples of how a plan that fits into God's plan works out over time as God guides our steps. God wants me to serve Him because His Son served me. Thanks to God, none of the obstacles that intervened in our lives have exhausted my determination to serve these men for His sake.

### Scriptural references
2 Timothy 2:2; Galatians 4:19; Colossians 1:28-29; Isaiah 53:3; Ephesians 4:12-13; 2 Corinthians 1:5; Proverbs 16:9

. . . . . . . . . . . . . . . . . . . . . . . . . . . . . . . . . . . . . . . . . . . . . . . . . . . . . . . . . . . . . . .

## Questions for reflection or discussion
. . . . . . . . . . . . . . . . . . . . . . . . . . . . . . . . . . . . . . . . . . . . . . . . . . . . . . . . . . . . . . .

What are your comments on this chapter?

What has been your personal experience with this topic?

Any Scriptures or principles discussed in this chapter you need to apply in your life?

# 8.
# Movement

............................

*"There is one body and one Spirit—just as you were called to
one hope when you were called— one Lord, one faith, one
baptism; one God and Father of all, who is over
all and through all and in all."*
*Ephesians 4:4-6*

## *Paul's perspective*

In the New Testament, the movement that develops with the followers of Jesus is described in the four Gospels. The book of Acts continues
to describe the movement as it becomes established in Jerusalem and
expands to the Gentiles with the apostle Paul's ministry. This movement
was not an outgrowth of an organization, religious institutions or church
buildings. On the contrary, the movement spread man-to-man throughout the Roman Empire after Jesus' resurrection. Because the followers of
Christ were persecuted, it largely spread person-to-person as an underground stealth movement.

For the first four hundred years following the resurrection, the following of Christ grew exponentially throughout the Roman Empire.
Then Roman Emperor Constantine, a converted believer, declared
Christianity would be the official religion of the Roman Empire. Every
Roman citizen was required to be a Christian; ironically, this event
marked the end to the exponential spread of Christianity throughout the
world. Starting with seeds of Reformation that first were planted around
1100 A.D., however, the institution of the Church emerged and has done
more good for humankind than any other institution on this planet.

History proves Christianity thrives in environments of persecution
and stagnates in environments of tolerance or legal enforcement. Putting it another way, the historic decree of Constantine effectively marked

the end of Christianity as a movement and the beginning of Christianity as another formalized world religion. However, the true movement of God has never ceased; because of persecution in Europe, the movement spread to early America. Today the movement's greatest advances are occurring in Africa, South America, and Asia, especially in China where it is growing exponentially and, in response to persecution, the movement often has gone underground.

In our city, a movement of businessmen developed not because of a plan but as a work of God over 25 years. A number of businessmen became discipled and began co-laboring together in a free-flowing process that grew uncontrolled, just as an organism would grow. God was doing many amazing things among the men, not because of a manmade plan or program, but simply as an outgrowth of the men's relationships with each other and the Lord.

At a point in time we began to call ourselves a movement, understanding it as something that was spontaneous and free flowing, not something we were trying to control, but rather something God was doing. Today, we don't want to hinder God's work, but desire only to watch it and get in line with what He is doing. He's bringing more and more men around us, not because we are trying to snare men, but because they come around us and like what they see. Men are drawn to us because they recognize we don't have a lot of rules, are not focused on the "shoulds" and "oughts" of life. They see us as more interested in loving each other, being around each other, and enjoying the company of wives, couples, families and friends.

As the spiritual family grows it causes a "movement mentality" to form among the Pauls, Timothys and their families. The movement which emerges is not an organization requiring a defined, formalized structure. However, because of its ministry nature, it will need some organization to support its events and tools.

The movement will require some administrative functions, but the administrative men do not become leaders because of their position, but usually provide leadership as core members of this initiative. Administrative men may be volunteers, or supported by the giving of members engaged in the movement or through other resources. The core members of this ministry are those who have the most maturity and commitment to the process. Outside of the core are men on the fringe that are somewhere in the process, men who are growing in their maturity and commitment to Christ.

The events and activities of the movement are limited to those things that support the Jesus-Paul-Timothy discipleship relationship. Again, the movement refers to this relationship as the JPT, which is the "brand" of this work. The majority of the one-on-one discipleship and activities of this Christ-centered mission take place in offices, restaurants and homes of those involved.

Men come into the movement from all different places. Many of the men who come into it have some organized church background. Very few come in with no personal church experience, so God uses the church in the process to prepare them for the next step of discipleship.

Typically, men who connect with this ministry attend church and discover they are empty and not growing because something is missing. There are many reasons for this, and I will not go into all of them. The major reason for this feeling of emptiness is actually that they are stuffed full. It's like eating a meal, chewing, chomping and swallowing, but never feel full or satisfied. Similarly, a person can listen to the messages in church and hold the information internally, without ever giving anything away – hoarding instead of sharing. In the movement, men learn to give their lives away to another man and this giving out from what God has given causes them to grow spiritually in a healthy fashion, filled and increasingly fulfilled.

Another thing that happens in churches is men can become so enamored with a particular minister or pastor. In clinging to and turning to a mere human, they sacrifice and miss out on a genuine, growing relationship with Jesus. When men come into the movement they realize the guys they meet are different. They are not following a man or a preacher, but seem to be bonded together in a common mission by their commitment to follow Christ. It is Christ that fills a man. Experiencing the saving life of Christ is a product of discipleship in this work. The apostle Paul writes in Romans 5:10 *"If when we were enemies we were reconciled to God through the death of His Son, much more, having been reconciled, we shall be saved by His life."* We receive "much more" than just forgiveness of our sins; we are to be "saved by his life."

The church is not a negative; it is a positive because it is a starting point for many men. The church can get a person started; a movement can help him get to the "much more" levels of spiritual maturity. Getting plugged into the JPT process drives the experience of what God fully intends for us in our eternal relationship with Him. Many men continue to be involved and benefit greatly from their relationship with organized religion once they are part of the discipleship movement.

There is a relational dynamic that has developed in the movement over time that is clearly a work of God. A core of a few men has emerged as a center of this movement that attracts more and more men. The movement has grown similar to the web of a spider. It starts with one at the center (Jesus), and over time others show up in the web attracted to the men – and to the presence of Jesus Christ in them.

A person comes into the movement and over time becomes equipped for discipleship. Looking back they realize that in the beginning they were really spiritual babies because they had no walk with Jesus, only a religious preference. As the light comes into men through the one-on-one JPT process, it changes their whole life. They become healthy, growing Christians because they become obedient in following Jesus' command to make disciples.

## Timothy's story

The movement began to impact my life two years after I was born again. I had found my way into a good, Bible-believing church. The early years of searching were painful and scary, but also exciting. I was like a man walking down a dark hallway, opening doors looking for light, the truth, which began to redirect my life. So for a couple of years, at age 40, I got educated through the teaching of a good preacher and a Sunday school teacher. However, I was hungry for more, particularly how to share my faith in the business world.

My world was still painful and full of difficulties. Everywhere I looked I was finding men I wanted to help who were lost and confused, but I did not know how to reach them. It was overwhelming. Business and legal problems were destroying the enthusiasm I once had for life. My wife was lost and wanted nothing to do with organized religion. She looked at me and the church crowd as "Holy Joes" to be avoided. The raging, angry arguments between us were draining the life and happiness out of me. I was miserable, joyless, discouraged and considering divorce.

About this time I began meeting with my newly found Paul. He and his wife came alongside my wife and me as a couple – and as friends. They would become our spiritual parents, comforting us and bringing sanity when we were acting insane. After a few years of this "one-on-one" process, I began to change from just a student of the Bible to a man having a walk with God, applying the Bible's truth to my life. Within the movement of like-minded men, I have been built up and equipped to live the life of a follower of Christ who is able to disciple others. This has brought me joy even when much of my life was out of control with problems.

I have been at this walk in the movement for more than 25 years. As a result, I have been healed from the life of a lost sinner I lived for 40 years. My marriage has been restored; my wife is walking alongside me, and both of us are following Christ. She is my greatest asset. All the suffering we experienced has been used by God for our good.

Today I have purpose, order, joy, gladness and hope in my life. Because of my involvement in concert with committed followers of Christ, I have grown over the last 25 years into the kind of man the Bible promises I can be. Through all of these years my Paul has walked alongside me and he is truly my spiritual father. Imitating my Paul, I have discipled a number of men who now find, as I have, purpose and companionship in the movement. I am continuing to grow as God and the world challenge me.

## Scripture references

Ephesians 4:4-6; Matthew 18:20; Romans 5:10; Romans 8:37-39; Matthew 28:19-20; John 3:1-36

## *Questions for reflection or discussion*

What are your comments on this chapter?

What has been your personal experience with this topic?

Any Scriptures or principles discussed in this chapter you need to apply in your life?

# Part II:

## *The Discipleship Process*

# 9.
# Prayer

................

*"Do not be anxious about anything, but in everything, by prayer
and petition, with thanksgiving, present your requests to God.
And the peace of God, which transcends all understanding, will
guard your hearts and your minds in Christ Jesus."*
Philippians 4:6-7

## Paul's perspective

Becoming a man of prayer is an outgrowth of my relationship with
God. Finding peace in this world we live in is a promise I expect God will
provide as I seek Him in prayer. Therefore, I have developed a conscious
communion with Jesus by continuously talking to Him, and this has
grown into a habit of just being with Him. Prayer – talking to the Father,
Jesus and the Holy Spirit – begins for me before my feet hit the floor
most every morning. Ongoing conversations will continue throughout
the day until my head hits the pillow and we say good night to each
other.

Some praying takes place in a restaurant meeting or driving down
the highway (with my eyes open). But I also have time on my knees in
my prayer closet, setting aside time to be exclusively with the Lord. I
need to humble myself before God and honor Him for who He is, for
everything, and remind myself that I am only His creation for Him to
do with as He pleases. Often I have no idea what to pray for or what to
ask God. At such times I turn to the Holy Spirit and ask Him to talk with
God about what I need. I am confident God knows what I need and will
provide. Sometimes we just need to be still and listen to God, realizing
that he is God.

The disciples asked Jesus to teach them to pray. He modeled prayer
for them by praying what we call "the Lord's Prayer" (in Luke 11:2-4).

He continues in teaching them about prayer by telling stories about prayer and making His points through these stories. First, Jesus modeled prayer; then He taught them about prayer. I try to follow the same pattern with my Timothy.

My relationship with Timothy began long before I met him. I prayed, asking God to give me a man and equip me with the character, skills and wisdom needed to disciple him. When the new Timothy is revealed, then my prayers for him become specific. Sometimes the Timothy is not someone I know and he just appears in my life. Other times he has been in my life for some time. I pray for men I know, asking God to quicken their spirit and give them a hunger for fellowship and God's Word.

Early in my one-on-one meetings with Timothy I ask him if I can pray for him, especially in the area of a need he may have expressed during our meeting. Usually, right there I will begin talking out loud to God about the need before we end the meeting. I like to pray at this time rather than say I will do so later – and then forget to pray. By presenting our requests to God and thanking Him, the process of modeling prayer begins before Timothy. Some Timothys are able to pray out loud, but in the beginning most are uncomfortable about praying. However, as they listen to me talk to God, they relax and eventually join me in our talks with God.

As Timothy and I meet weekly or biweekly as our schedules allow, we develop a list of things for which to pray. I keep this dated list, or prayer log, and periodically we go back and look at the list. Seeing how God has answered prayers is meaningful in my teaching Timothy to pray. In addition, I like to use a prayer card from the *Operation Timothy* books called a "Ten Most Wanted" prayer card (available through www.cbmc.com). We use this card to pray for the lost, for men to disciple, and for workers and laborers to become engaged in the cause of Christ. As requests are answered, Timothy begins to see that God truly is hearing and responding to our prayers.

I often pray over the phone with men when there is a need. A lot of my meetings with men are concluded with a prayer of thanksgiving and petition. With today's technology I sometimes answer an email or text with a written prayer. Living my life before Timothy with an attitude of active prayer is how I am striving to teach prayer – modeling prayer to provide an example. In addition, I am thankful for men who write books on prayer. Two books that have influenced me are *Power through Prayer* by E.M. Bounds, and *If You Will Ask* by Oswald Chambers.

Passing books and CDs on to Timothys is something I make a habit of doing. Men learn best out of their natural learning grid. Some are visual and will eagerly read books to learn. Others are verbal, preferring to hear teachings from CDs. Knowing Timothy's learning style is important, so I give him materials he will use and learn from as he becomes a man of prayer.

## Timothy's story

When I became involved in one-on-one discipleship, my Paul began modeling prayer for me. I really did not know how to pray. He seemed so comfortable just talking to God. After a while I began talking to God just like my Paul talked to Him. As a result I have experienced God answering all manner of prayer requests: asking God to bring lost men and women into the Kingdom, as well as asking Him to send me men to disciple, and that these men would become mature in the process to the point of discipling another man. These have become powerful examples of answered prayer in my life.

Early in the JPT (Jesus-Paul-Timothy) process my Paul taught me the value of praying daily for every aspect of my life, including my marriage, children and grandchildren. This has become a priority with me. When my first granddaughter was in her mother's womb, I began asking God to draw her to Him and bring her into the Kingdom. Around the age of three she began to have a healthy interest in God, asking me to read her Bible stories. Each summer we attended a spiritual vacation week with her family and she continued to be interested in the spiritual teaching for her age group during the week. When she was six we went to the vacation week, even though her parents were separated and headed toward divorce. She seemed to be adjusting and having a good time despite the troubled marriage.

During that week children and adults were being baptized in the river. The tradition started a number of years ago when one on my Timothys asked me if I would baptize him. Many from our group that attends every year came and watched, and thus a tradition began. A fond memory that I have of river baptism was a story told to me by my father. In about 1915, he was baptized in the river after church by his own father.

While at our spiritual vacation week, my granddaughter, my wife and I were swimming in the rapids upstream. It was a long walk back to the part of the river where the baptisms take place. As we started back, my granddaughter asked us if she could be baptized. We stopped and asked questions regarding her understanding of salvation and baptism. Her answers were right on and together we prayed as she invited Jesus into her life as Savior.

Her father and mother were at the baptism site. She said she wanted her father to do the actual baptism, and he did. It is something I shall never forget. In my mind God had answered my prayer that began before she was born. He blessed me by allowing me to be intimately involved in her accepting Christ. My prayer for her now is that she will walk in the truth of God's Word as she navigates this uncertain world she is growing up in.

Because my Paul modeled prayer, I have become a man of prayer imitating what I observed him doing. Today I am doing the same for other men, hoping they too will become men of prayer.

### Scripture references

Philippians 4:6-7; Luke 11:1-13; James 5:16; Matthew 9:37-38; Psalm 46:10; John 15:7; 3 John 4

. . . . . . . . . . . . . . . . . . . . . . . . . . . . . . . . . . . . . . . . . . . . . . . . . . . . . . . . . . . . . . .

## Questions for reflection or discussion

. . . . . . . . . . . . . . . . . . . . . . . . . . . . . . . . . . . . . . . . . . . . . . . . . . . . . . . . . . . . . . .

What are your comments on this chapter?

What has been your personal experience with this topic?

Any Scriptures or principles discussed in this chapter you need to apply in your life?

# 10.
# The Word

............................

*"All Scripture is God-breathed and is useful for teaching, rebuking, correcting and training in righteousness, so that the man of God may be thoroughly equipped for every good work."*
Timothy 3:16-17

## Paul's perspective

The Scriptures are useful for showing a man the path of salvation he needs to walk. They show us when we are off the path and how to get back on the path. The Word also shows a man how to stay on the path of following God's plan for our lives. Without the Word as my truth and guide for life, I am dominated by my sinful mind that is hostile to God and cannot please Him.

The Word of God should be read, listened to, studied, memorized and meditated on by Timothy. If these disciplines are practiced with dependence on the Holy Spirit, Timothy will begin to communicate with God through His Word. It is through the Spirit that a man becomes empowered to know the mind of Christ. "This provides direction and guidance so a man can deal with the complexities of life in a godly manner" (Walt Henrichsen).

Teaching the Word to Timothy is critical for his spiritual maturity. There are many good ministries effective in teaching the Word in an instructional format. This type of teaching usually occurs in group Bible studies or through in-class, lecture-type formats. The end result of such instructional teaching, however, may only be an intellectual experience.

My approach is a life-on-life experience with the Word between Timothy and me. Over and over he hears my testimony of how the living Word is impacting me and changing my life. He sees the Word alive in my life. It is often difficult for people to grasp how the Word can work out in their own life unless they see this happening in someone else's life.

In the discipleship process, Timothy sees there is a life going on in me that is connected to God through his Word. He observes my walk, listens to my love for Christ, and hears what Christ has done in my life, not from a teaching format but in a life-to-life manner. Over time, Timothy understands and realizes the Word is alive, real and changing his own life. This life-on-life approach to the Scriptures is quite different from the instructional approach.

When I befriend a man who will be faithful to meet with me, I begin praying for this potential Timothy to become willing and eager to look at the Word. The one-on-one discipleship process is based on God's truth found in the Bible. The Scriptures serve as our teacher and resource for all truth by which the man of God needs to live his life.

Men with Christian religious backgrounds are generally familiar with the Bible; most of them recognize it is an important book for a Christian to study. But the secular man has little, if any, knowledge about the Bible, so with him I am careful not to suggest too soon the idea of studying it. With both types of men I approach studying the Bible by using an *Operation Timothy* study book (available on *www.CBMC.com*) that first addresses the credibility of the Bible. Here I get a sense of the man's preconceived ideas about the Bible and use this information to determine how I should begin to approach its truths with him.

The Bible is not just a book. It's a library of 66 books, written by 40 different authors from all walks of life, in three languages over a period of 1,500 years. It contains a simple, consistent theme, yet men can study it over their lifetime and still never succeed in mastering it.

Our initial study of the contents of the Bible starts with the basics of who Jesus is and His gift of salvation to us. In the first booklet of the *Operation Timothy* study series, the Scriptures we will be studying are given as part of the text. It usually takes three to five months to finish this book. With the rest of the *Operation Timothy* booklets, however, it is necessary to use the Bible for locating the Scripture passages we will be studying. This helps him in becoming familiar with how the Bible is organized.

The best situation for our Bible study is for Paul and Timothy to use the same version of the Bible. It helps if this version is compatible with the study materials we are using. Often I buy Timothy a study Bible that has many good reference tools included with the text, and I usually spend time with him on how to cross-reference, use the commentaries and a concordance.

My prayer is for God to give Timothy a hunger to retain the Word in his heart through Scripture memory. God speaks to the man who has the Word in him by the power of the Holy Spirit. Scriptures will be brought into this man's mind so he can apply them to the circumstances of his life, and as he puts God's Word into practice, his faith grows.

I encourage Timothy to get into the Word daily and stay in it consistently. When he is ready and equipped in his understanding of the basics of the Bible, I will encourage him to develop a habit of reading it through cover-to-cover. In my own experience, I started in the New Testament, which I found more interesting and easier to understand. Then I began to read the Old Testament. Over the years I have read through the Bible a number of times using different versions. As our JPT (Jesus-Paul-Timothy) relationship matures and we begin walking together more like peers, I take him to the Bible to show him what God is teaching me in my daily time with Him. The Word is our source of wisdom, truth and knowledge. The Scriptures and the Holy Spirit are our teachers. Through this process, Timothy and I become intimate with Christ and build an intimate, trusting relationship with each other.

## Timothy's story

As a new Christian getting into the *Operation Timothy* study with my Paul, I was very troubled with life in general. I wore a lot of hats. I put on the hat of a businessman most days. At home I was a father and husband. I wore the gardener's hat when I took care of the yard. With all the hats I put on, I had become exhausted and tired with life.

My Paul said that I needed to look at Matthew 11:28-30, *"Come to me, all you who are weary and burdened, and I will give you rest. Take my yoke upon you and learn from me, for I am gentle and humble in heart, and you will find rest for your souls. For my yoke is easy and my burden is light."*

I remember reading these verses and finding so much comfort in them. From these verses I discovered new things about Jesus. Previously, I had regarded Him as a God that was standing there with a hammer in His hand, and I had to move fast enough so as not to get hammered. He was a God, in my view, who was out to get me.

However, in these verses I began to see Him as a loving God who had my best interests at heart. Discovering these character qualities made me feel as if He understood. I learned that if I would call to Him with my trials, He would give me rest. I had never before received His rest nor did I understand what His rest was like. In the beginning, as I began to hear the Word of God, it was as if supernaturally Jesus was speaking the words directly to me. When He said, *"Come to me all you who are weary and burdened,"* I felt as if He was speaking to me. Little by little I began to experience His healing touch.

When I would start feeling overwhelmed with life, I would come back to Him and tell Him I was coming to Him as He told me to do. He healed me slowly, little by little, from the overpowering pressures of the world. A world that would get up on top of me, a world I could not control. I learned to trust God through His Word and not just trust something that was imaginary. These were the true words Jesus had said, words that were real and He wanted me to trust and rely on: *"Come to me, all you who are weary and burdened, and I will give you rest."* This was my greatest need. Realizing I could receive rest from God was an amazing part of my new life and it came from developing a meaningful relationship with the Word of God.

## Scripture references

2 Timothy 3:16-17; Hebrews 4:12; Romans 12:2; Psalms 119:105; 1 Corinthians 2:13-14; Romans 8:6-8; Matthew 11:28-30.

. . . . . . . . . . . . . . . . . . . . . . . . . . . . . . . . . . . . . . . . . . . . . . . . . . . . . . . . . . . . .

## *Questions for reflection or discussion*

. . . . . . . . . . . . . . . . . . . . . . . . . . . . . . . . . . . . . . . . . . . . . . . . . . . . . . . . . . . . .

What are your comments on this chapter?

What has been your personal experience with this topic?

Any Scriptures or principles discussed in this chapter you need to apply in your life?

# 11.
# Strategy
.....................

*"Greater love has no one than this, that he*
*lay down his life for his friends."*
John 15:13

## Paul's perspective

Jesus modeled a strategy of developing friendships with people. As he went about His travels, Jesus would sit and talk to strangers, outcasts and undesirables as He did with the Samaritan woman at the well, or drop by their home as He did with Mary and Martha. Jesus obviously had an attitude of laying down His life for his friends. We are to be servants of Jesus, but He chose to call us His friends. From His perspective, we are His friends.

When I first meet a person, my initial strategy, like that of Jesus, is to think, *"Could this be someone I could have a healthy friendship with?"* With a little encouragement on my part, a friendship often begins to develop. Using my talents, interests and expertise to assist others is an effective way of making friends with the lost. The use of golf, movies, investments, card games, hunting, fishing, camping, marital advice, and business interests, are some activities that one can employ to develop common ground. These types of activities are often where relationships with nonbelievers develop and lifestyle evangelism begins to take place.

Most of my male relationships are born out of felt needs. If someone feels I am competent in an area where they are interested in developing competency – and I am in fact competent – then the basis for a friendship is established. I was a professional tennis teacher for 20 years and people were always interested in getting my help with tips, lessons, and playing in matches. As a means of establishing friendships and maintaining my enjoyment of the game, I put together matches and tournaments in my neighborhood. Many friendships were established through this strategy.

Developing a friendship takes commitment, time, unconditional love, and acceptance. Relationships blossom when character, honesty, integrity and forgiveness are lived out in front of a person. A man with whom you can share personal things out of your life, and feel secure that person will not judge or defame you in any way, is a safe person. Being that kind of a person is a goal of my friendship with a man.

The attitude of loving people and accepting them is important, whether or not they ever become followers of Christ. All people are important and valuable to God in fulfilling His purposes and in bringing about His plans. We are not privy to how He will use that person or what their life is going to be like. I was once challenged to count how many nonbelievers I thought would call me their friend. At that time, unfortunately, I had caused considerable relationship damage among nonbelievers with my religious talk and behavior. So I could count very few. My religious spouting and Bible thumping had driven away a lot of people. Therefore, I had to learn to die to my religious behavior around nonbelievers so I could connect with them. Becoming a loving friend to those who are not in a relationship with Christ is now my goal, even if it may bring me criticism or condemnation in the eyes of those believers who don't share my willingness to befriend the lost.

The introduction of the spiritual aspect will begin slowly in many relationships. When they are ready, my goal is to share the Word of God with my friend and observe how it brings about transformation in our lives. The spiritual aspect of our friendship can last a lifetime and it brings for me rewarding memories of time invested in another's life.

I model befriending people for Timothy by bringing him around my unbelieving friends. Developing his own particular attributes that will appeal to a nonbeliever's felt needs is important for Timothy in finding men he can meet with and disciple. His skill at becoming a loving friend of lost sinners is a critical aspect of developing Christ-like character. It is here where he will die to his judgmental attitudes and learn to truly and unconditionally love God's greatest creation – people.

Because I don't know what God has planned for people, but know He created us to be relational beings, my strategy is to remain open to befriend everyone with whom I come in contact. It is through friendships and by loving people as they are that God builds the ministry of one-on-one discipleship in my life.

## Timothy's story

I first met a man who ultimately became my Timothy when he came by my office to show me a real estate deal. He was a driven, outgoing sales type. His success seemed built around his willingness to serve his clients by searching for whatever they would be interested in and helping them buy it or sell it. As we began to discuss deals, I invited him to visit a nonreligious men's lunch that was held every two weeks at our office. I explained that the meetings involved discussions about life issues of interest to men. He had some religious background but little interest in spiritual matters, so this lunch meeting was a good fit for him.

For five years we continued to talk business, and he came to the office discussion group on a regular basis. We talked with each other about our lives, both past and present. Because we lived on opposite sides of town, it was difficult getting together unless it was planned.

He lived with a woman who was his business partner. My wife and I met with them occasionally for a meal and they seemed willing to have a somewhat superficial relationship. They were both very motivated to succeed and had a busy social schedule with a large number of acquaintances he called "friends."

His large, dysfunctional genetic family burdened him with many hurtful issues. He often shared his concerns with me. He was in a partnership with some rather ruthless men and a lot of his cash was in jeopardy. This situation had become a great burden, crushing the life out of him. He did not know what to do. I thought about asking him to study the Bible with me, but he had told me he was feeling pressure to read all of his business and professional-related materials and just finding time to keep up with that was overwhelming. Adding Bible study to that list seemed unrealistic.

One day, after five years of meeting together in our biweekly office discussion lunch, he asked me how one could know what the truth was. I suggested we have coffee and discuss this question. I met him a couple of days later. At this meeting he agreed to examine the Bible with me as a source of truth. We started using the *Operation Timothy Study Guide* (available through www.cbmc.com) and he was faithful to show up for our meetings. After a couple of months of meeting and examining the

Scriptures, talking about Jesus and our need for forgiveness of our sins, he admitted his need for salvation. We were sitting in a coffee shop when he invited Christ into his life.

Since that day I have spent a lot of time with him. He loves to be around the fellowship of the men's movement. His desire to grow spiritually is evidenced by his interest in spiritual teachings. He listens to spiritual recordings and has read through the Bible cover to cover. The woman he lives with has become more and more interested in spiritual matters and has attended numerous events with my wife and me. We also have taken a couple of trips together with them. They did a Crown Financial Study with some other couples and as a result have developed a desire to manage their money according to Biblical principles.

This process with this Timothy has been going on for about 12 years. At his own pace (not mine) he is moving through the process of coming out of a life of darkness into a life with Christ. He has become a witness to his sphere of influence and has a strategy to find a man he can befriend and lead to the truth of the Bible.

## Scripture references
John 15:13; John 13:34-35; Matthew 11:19; John 15:15

..........................................................................

## Questions for reflection or discussion

..........................................................................

What are your comments on this chapter?

What has been your personal experience with this topic?

Any Scriptures or principles discussed in this chapter you need to apply in your life?

# 12.
# Selection

·····················

*"And the things you have heard me say in the
presence of many witnesses entrust to reliable
men who will also be qualified to teach others."*
2 Timothy 2:2

## Paul's perspective

Jesus was looking for men into whom He could impart His life and
the truth. These men were to be left with the discipleship ministry of
teaching the next generation. Jesus began His ministry by selecting some
of His disciples and taking them to His home in John 1:35-41 to show
them how He lived:

*"The next day John was there again with two of his disciples. When
he saw Jesus passing by, he said, 'Look, the Lamb of God.' When the two
disciples heard him say this, they followed Jesus. Turning around, Jesus saw
them following and asked, 'What do you want?' They said, 'Rabbi' (which
means Teacher), 'where are you staying?' 'Come,' he replied, 'and you will
see.' So they went and saw where he was staying, and spent that day with
him. It was about the tenth hour. Andrew, Simon Peter's brother, was one
of the two who heard what John had said and who had followed Jesus. The
first thing Andrew did was to find his brother Simon and tell him, 'We have
found the Messiah' (that is, the Christ). And he brought him to Jesus."*

Jesus had no plan "B." These men were His only plan for taking the
Gospel message to the world. They spent the next three years listening to
Him and observing Him in the everyday aspects of his life. Their train-
ing came from observing His life.

The man who discipled me took me into his home, and it was there
that I began to see a living, breathing model of Christianity. This is a very
important principle of the one-on-one discipleship process. Hospitality

is defined as making strangers feel welcome in our home. When God sends me a man, I like to take him into my home and let him observe how I live. For me, Christianity is not confined to a church building, or merely a place where I go. True Christianity is demonstrated through the living of one's life, most especially in the home. I want men to notice a difference in my home and how our family carries out their lives as followers of Jesus Christ. Timothy needs to see how I respond when things are going well, as well as how I handle failure. We meet men in the marketplace, but it is in the home where Christ is most clearly demonstrated because that is the place where our lives are truly and honestly lived out.

For me, finding a person to disciple is best started by prayer, asking God to send me a man that I can meet with regularly. In gathering men it is important to select a certain kind of man. He should be Faithful, Available and Teachable: a FAT man. I pray for God to send me men who will be FAT men, qualified to carry the process to the next generation.

The Bible records no evidence that Paul discipled any women. I only meet one-on-one with men in the discipleship process. I believe women are most effective in discipling women, and men don't always relate to the ways of women. Accordingly, I don't disciple women. This also avoids any potential opposite-sex attraction problems.

From my perspective, men fall into two categories – those with a religious belief system, and secular men with little or no religious background. The secular person is more of a spiritual blank page and presents a lot of challenges for me as I walk with him and he learns about God. It takes a lot longer to order his life according to the wisdom of God and His Word, but at the same time he is free from the baggage of denominational religion. I have discovered men like this are more likely to reproduce the one-on-one discipleship model than the religious man.

The religious person may have a grasp of the basics of the Biblical Word and likely will have adopted some denominational values and behavior. Yet these learned mindsets and behaviors often hinder him from becoming a one-on-one discipler of others. Some of these men view their job as inviting men to church, then letting the pastor or teachers do the rest. Still, many dedicated disciplemakers have come from religious backgrounds. I have discipled many men who have set aside their religiosity and focused on the one-on-one process.

God looks at the heart of a man. A heart for others is the most critical ingredient in the selection process.

## Timothy's story

I am a visual learner. For me life is best modeled, since modeling through example probably has the greatest impact on my beliefs. My most influential models have been my parents, teachers/coaches, friends, culture, pastors, Sunday school teachers, etc. From the modeling of others I developed my worldview, values and beliefs.

Through church I was introduced to spiritual things early in life. That influence lasted until junior high. We stopped attending church and then it was gone. However, some foundation was laid during those formative years. I was not opposed to God or Jesus Christ; I just did not see any need for them in my life.

It wasn't until I was 20 that I was drawn to Christ out of need and came into a relationship with Him. He then began to take on value and relevance in my life. A man by the name of Paul invested about six months of his life in me during my first year as a follower of Christ. He took me into his home and played racquetball with me. Being in his home, I had the opportunity to see how he actually lived life with his family. I believe his greatest issue at that time was dealing with a learning-disabled son. Despite this challenging circumstance, his home appeared peaceful and well-managed. In other words, it seemed nice and neat, and I felt this man had a genuine love for Christ. After our time together he suggested I attend his Sunday school class.

At this point I had come full circle and was back in the church, which seemed normal, something good for me that I should be doing. However, it was my only spiritual time. So the model for me at this time was to go to church and let the church feed me. This went on for six years. By then I had two children and was struggling in my marriage, with my finances, and with understanding how to properly lead in my home.

I stopped going to church, resulting in no spiritual activity in my life, and began longing for some fellowship. About this time I met a man named Jay who invited me to a lunch and subsequently to a bi-weekly men's group. I went mainly to fill my need for fellowship. It was there that I was introduced to life-on-life, one-on-one discipleship.

The man who began to disciple me was active in his church and handled our time together like a program. We went through some discipleship materials called *Operation Timothy (OT,* available at www.cbmc.com). Our time together had some relational aspects to it, but after our twelve meetings we did not meet any more. And I proceeded to do likewise, treating the process like a program while meeting with my initial man because that was what had been modeled for me. I was enjoying the fellowship with the man I was meeting with and the men's group, and felt involved in something meaningful to Christ.

About a year into my time with the men's group, Jay spoke about a man he was spending time with named Dave. Dave sounded like a man who took a genuine interest in people, so I asked to meet him. After my initial meeting with Dave I was drawn to his authenticity and it felt like he genuinely had an interest in me. So I pursued Dave and asked if he would meet with me and be my spiritual father. He agreed to both. We began our relationship in 1988, when I was 28. We did not go back through OT but met almost weekly for about two years. He listened as I shared my heart regarding my life issues, and we discussed Scriptures as they related to my life.

As Dave invested in my life, he brought me into his home where I witnessed his life. I have learned more from observing Dave than most anything he has ever spoken to me. I watched how he loved his wife, trained his children, dealt with family issues (marriage and children), and related with other men and couples. I also saw how he handled his money and spent time with Christ.

Dave has walked with me through a divorce, children from a broken home and the issues that followed, as well as an adulterous relationship (for which he did not judge me, but treated me with grace and unconditional love). We also walked through my re-marrying, getting fired and laid off, becoming the father of two more children, and working to maintain a meaningful relationship with my two adult children.

God has used Dave to fill the gaps my parents left. Dave has helped me learn how to love Christ, to love my wife and relate to her, to get my finances in order, to feed myself spiritually, and train my two boys. He continues to model life through Christ and because of his modeling, life-on-life relationships have become a way of life for me. Every person that God brings into my life I view through a life-on-life lens. In other words, people are of great importance and I am looking to God for how He may choose to use me.

### Scripture references
2 Timothy 2:2; Isaiah 43:4; John 1:35-41; 1Samuel 16:9; 1 Peter 3:1-7

. . . . . . . . . . . . . . . . . . . . . . . . . . . . . . . . . . . . . . . . . . . . . . . . . . . . . . . . . . . . . . .

## *Questions for reflection or discussion*
. . . . . . . . . . . . . . . . . . . . . . . . . . . . . . . . . . . . . . . . . . . . . . . . . . . . . . . . . . . . . . .

What are your comments on this chapter?

What has been your personal experience with this topic?

Any Scriptures or principles discussed in this chapter you need to apply in your life?

# 13.
# Transparency and Humility

································································

*"God opposes the proud but gives grace to the humble."*
James 4:6b

## Paul's perspective

There is no exact formula for spiritual growth that leads to spiritual maturity, but humility and transparency provide fertile ground for the process. In the New Testament book of James, the Scriptures tell us that God "opposes the proud, but gives grace to the humble," and if we humble ourselves, then God will lift us up. In other words, He grows us and matures us spiritually as we humble ourselves.

The process of developing transparency and humility is very difficult for many men because they must begin to verbalize their shortcomings, weakness and sinfulness. This requires a willingness to say, "This is who I really am and this is what's going on in my life," and thus opening up and becoming vulnerable. This usually begins with the Paul being vulnerable first to serve as an example for Timothy. As he does so, in time Timothy feels free and safe enough to become vulnerable himself.

This is a very slow process and involves getting to the truth and exposing the façade. At some point Timothy realizes that truth is a person, Jesus Christ, who said, "I am the way and the truth." As the light of Christ exposes a man and shines the truth on the reality of his sinfulness, the man becomes aware Christ will take him where He wants him to go and he can trust Him.

A story that illustrates this need involves a young boy who awakens in the middle of the night and cries out to his dad. The boy tells his dad that he is scared and fearful. His dad consoles the boy, telling him to "just trust God to keep you safe." The boy replies to his dad, "But I really need God with skin on." When a man comes into another man's life, it is like

God coming into his life with skin on. He is someone who has walked farther down the road and thus is able to give the man the encouragement, hope and exhortation necessary for the leap to spiritual maturity, enabling him to grow and eventually to start helping another person.

The process of humility starts with transparency and could be compared to the difference your senses experience when going from darkness into light. It's like waking up in a dark room with daylight approaching. At first we can see nothing, but little by little we begin noticing objects in the room becoming visible and more defined as our eyes adjust. The longer we are exposed to the intensifying light making its way into the room, the more we are able to see.

Similarly, the fact is that men live in the light, but they walk as blind men in darkness in the matters of their souls because their souls have not been awakened. Men live, unwittingly, as though the lights are off, preferring to live in the shadows, in the secret places of the mind. These are places where the mind lingers on thoughts we would not want anyone else to know are there, tucked away in the believed comfort of elusive privacy. Ironically, many times they are unaware their behavior betrays their thoughts. We have many secrets about ourselves and secret places within us that we have not shared with anyone and for good reason – they would betray what we want people to believe about who we are and how we want others to perceive us. In the Timothy discipling process, over time a man learns it is OK and safe to share his secrets with his Paul, just as Paul becomes transparent and real with him.

In time, discussions with Timothy become more "real" and less self-protective. As I talk with Timothy about my own secrets and darkness, he then becomes willing to share his own struggles and God begins to expose the darkness that served as his basis of life prior to this light entering into his soul. He starts to allow me into his soul and I let him into mine. It is not long before we become soul mates, in a sense.

This transparency and humility precede our spiritual growth as we humble ourselves before God and another man. By nature, men are guarded in close, personal relationships with other men and thus their spiritual growth remains immature or at best, limited to outward, flippant expressions without addressing real inner, spiritual battles.

Discipling others is humbling work. It imposes a retracing of my own circumstances that lead me out of the darkness and into the

Lord's marvelous light. I accept being involved in a work He is under-taking, the transformation of a man into a vessel in whom God can live and be seen. My pride only gets in the way of God's work, so I must and will be humbled in the process as I seek to align my will with His. My surrender in becoming humble initiates the process as I begin to expose my true nature, that of a fallen man who can do nothing without Jesus. As I reveal my struggles and failures to Timothy, he starts to feel free to accept and reveal his own struggles and failures. This type of dialogue separates discipling from all other forms of self-improvement. In opening up, I begin the process of sharing the wisdom God has shown me as I learn to walk with Him, trusting Him for all things. Transparency and humility on my part are the fuel that powers the relationship-building between Jesus, Paul and Timothy (JPT).

## Timothy's story

I had been a follower of Christ for 11 years and active in the one-on-one discipleship, Jesus, Paul, Timothy process. This is my story of how I was humiliated, broken, and in due time lifted up as I have become more and more transparent – more and more the Lord's instrument.

My wife and I drove to San Antonio and spent the weekend trying to enjoy the beautiful Riverwalk area of downtown San Antonio. We had hoped the judge would let me stay out of prison while my appeal on a white-collar crime conviction was heard. He said we had no chance of success and I learned that 95% of all appeals in Federal Court are turned down. I checked into the Federal Prison Camp and my wife drove home. She cried all the way home, a couple of hundred miles, and began her struggle with loneliness. She also had the added burden of taking over what was left of my business, which would be her primary source of income.

Ninety percent of the camp's population was comprised of drug-related offenders. They called me a swindler. According to them, my crime was worse than theirs because what they did made people happy. To them, drugs were good and I was the bad guy, who in their mind swindled little old ladies. This was an upside-down world. I accepted a prison job as a janitor with a starting pay of only $5.35 *per month*, not per hour.

When this all started, a friend God had sent to encourage me pointed out a Bible verse, one that became my verse of hope. The verse said, "humble yourself under God's mighty hand and in due time he will lift you up." At this point, I had no idea that my humbling was to be so extensive.

While in prison, I focused on my ministry of discipleship to men. I took the time to improve my mind and my physical condition. After about a year and a half in prison, the 5th Circuit Court of Appeals heard my case and overturned all 15 of the savings & loan transaction related counts against me. It turned out that our accountants and lawyers were right and the regulators, FBI and federal prosecutors, in their zeal to convict, had attempted to make up some new law. Most men come out of prison angry and bitter. After three years I came out of prison humbled and broken, but still confident that God, in His own way and in His own timing, was reconciling matters in my life.

In 1994, when I reported to prison, I had no money and 14 separate legal and financial issues, including fines, taxes, restitution, past due accounts, lawsuits, convictions and judgments. My experience with our Federal legal system is behind me now. Today, all of the claims have been resolved. God has "lifted me up in due time" as the Bible promised. Now I am a free man, again selling real estate and enjoying my discipleship ministry with men. My marriage is healing and my golf handicap has risen to double digits. Contrary to what you may have heard, Federal Prison Camp is not a country club and there are no golf courses.

Three businessmen I met and began discipling in prison are among my best friends. These men have become as transparent with me as I am with them, and they share my passion for discipling men. We met in an environment surrounded by angry, unhappy, nasty, mean, bitter, hopeless, scary men who had not experienced the saving grace of Jesus in their lives. When we got together we enjoyed talking about how we found contentment while our few personal possessions were contained in an 8" x 12" x 36" locker. Our contentment was based not on what we possessed, but on our relationship with Jesus.

At one time I thought that trusting my life to God would insure me a life of success as the world defines it. Not so. In the eyes of the world I am a convicted felon, a failure. In this sense the only thing that trusting my life to God has insured is that He has been with me every humbling, painful step of the way. He is a wonderful comfort in times of struggle and a great source of counsel for the difficult decisions of life.

## Scripture references

James 4:6-10; Proverbs 3:5-6; Proverbs 3:34; 2 Corinthians 12:9-10; John 14:6; Acts 8:32-33a; Acts 26:17b-18: Philippians; 4:12; 1 Peter 5:5b-6

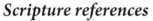

# Questions for reflection or discussion

What are your comments on this chapter?

What has been your personal experience with this topic?

Any Scriptures or principles discussed in this chapter you need to apply in your life?

# 14.
# Mentoring and Coaching

································································

*"We loved you so much that we were delighted to share*
*with you not only the Gospel of God but our lives as well,*
*because you had become so dear to us."*
1 Thessalonians 2:8

## *Paul's perspective*

Mentoring and coaching are popular subjects today. They are powerful tools that can be used for developing a person's competency, as a vehicle for moving up the corporate ladder, and for achieving success. The business, educational, and even the religious communities have labeled these two strategies as important ways to develop personal and spiritual maturity. However, discipling a man is not the same as mentoring or coaching a man. Discipleship is a spiritual process, and mentoring and coaching are secular processes. Understanding the differences is important to both Timothy and Paul as they share their lives with each other.

In the mentoring/coaching process, the mentor is the example and authority. Using his own philosophy, the coach **instructs** the student as to how he should go about performing the various things being taught. The mentor models his beliefs and the student can follow or selectively reject the examples being given. ***The power to make changes comes out of the student's own desires, energy and resources.*** If the student chooses to reject the coach's instructions, often the relationship ends.

However, in the discipleship process Paul **models** what the Lord has taught him. Timothy can follow Paul's lead or he can go his own way. As opposed to the mentoring/coaching process, the power to change and mature is not born out of self-centered desire. Change comes from the indwelling Holy Spirit of Christ. Paul observes this work of God in the life of Timothy and encourages him to stay on the path.

Both Paul and Timothy are learners in the one-on-one discipleship process because they learn from each other. I can't begin to describe the degree and depth of the things I have personally gleaned and learned from my various Timothys. The common focus between the two men in these roles is mutual growth. Discipleship therefore is a mutually beneficial relationship.

In most instances, the mentor doesn't learn much from the one he is mentoring since he is a top-down guy, meaning the mentor is in a position of authority over the mentoree (also called the mentee or protégé). In contrast, discipleship is a give-and-take process, in which both parties are learning. Timothy learns and shares from his perspective, and Paul learns and shares from his perspective. The only difference is that Paul has been walking with the Lord longer, traveled farther down the path, and having been discipled, often may have more experience in a matter.

The chart below is designed to assist in understanding the differences between mentoring/coaching and discipleship.

## Contrasting Mentoring and Discipleship

[Assumes all relationships are one-on-one as Teacher/Student vs. Paul/Timothy]

| MENTORING/COACHING | vs. | DISCIPLESHIP |
|---|---|---|
| **Relationship Contrasts** | | |
| Friend | vs. | Family |
| A sage advisor | vs. | A follower and a pupil |
| Teaching | vs. | Walking through life |
| Mentee following mentor | vs. | Modeling the following of Christ |
| **Authority Contrasts** | | |
| Selectively following advice | vs. | Obedience to God's Word |
| Teacher is the authority | vs. | Christ is the authority |
| Teacher exhibits strength | vs. | Teacher and student exhibit weakness |

| Behavior Contrasts | | |
| --- | --- | --- |
| If it makes sense do it | vs. | Follow me and do as I do |
| Advice and control | vs. | Responsibility and accountability |
| Promotes pride | vs. | Promotes humility |
| Result Contrasts | | |
| This may help me | vs. | I am responsible to disciple others [4th generation reproduction] |
| Purpose of personal maturity | vs. | Purpose of maturity in Christ |
| Focus varies | vs. | Focused on character, community and competency |
| Focused on teaching theories | vs. | Focused on how to trust God |

(Note: a more complete list of these differences is provided in Appendix I)

Discipleship is God's plan for the development of spiritual maturity. Mentoring/coaching are not bad tools in the secular sense. However, they are worldly processes, not spiritual ones. Mentoring and coaching are effective secular means of achieving secular success. On the other hand, discipleship is a spiritual process, where transformation takes place within the follower of Christ, enabling him to become a man with a totally new perspective on how to live and discern God's will for his life.

## Timothy's story

In my life, I have had both a mentor and a Paul. I was mentored by an older businessman. After nine years of working under him and being mentored by him, I ventured out into the business world and became like him – a very successful businessman.

Six years later, not long after I became a new Christian, a man came into my life and began the process of discipling me. Mentoring was great for the business side of my life, but my Paul modeled a life that was lived for Christ, for which I am eternally thankful. The major difference is that with the mentor I was looking for someone to help me in my career. He came from the top-down perspective, however, advising what I should do to become as successful as he was.

The guy who discipled me was like the father figure I never had. Initially, he treated me like a friend, modeling and imparting to me so many things about how to live my life. These were things I did not know. In the New Testament books of 1 and 2 Timothy and 1 Thessalonians, I could see the heart of Paul laboring for people. My Paul made me feel dear to him as though he were giving me his life. He was like an open book. I could speak to him about my frailties, shortcomings and dreams because I knew he was praying for me and not judging me. I have spent many years attempting to do the same for other men who have come into my life. He modeled how to strive to be successful in terms of Christ-like living.

For me, mentoring and discipling require entirely different mentalities. Mentoring *taught* me how to make money. My Paul *demonstrated* to me how to live out my life for and with Christ.

### Scripture reference
1 Thessalonians 2:8; 1 John 2:1; Romans 12:2

....................................................................
## Questions for reflection or discussion
....................................................................

What are your comments on this chapter?

What has been your personal experience with this topic?

Any Scriptures or principles discussed in this chapter you need to apply in your life?

# 15.
# Encouragement and
# Giving Grace

*"God opposes the proud but gives grace to the humble.*
*Humble yourselves, therefore, under God's mighty hand,*
*that he may lift you up in due time."*
1 Peter 5:5b-6

## Paul's perspective

God has given me grace and unconditional forgiveness for my rebellion against Him. In a similar way, I should extend the same grace to Timothy for the transgressions I am able to discern in his life. Judgment of Timothy will not encourage him or me. Instead I give him unmerited acceptance for his faults. Timothy is not my project; rather he is God's man to change and mold as He pleases. If any fruitful changes are to be made in Timothy, they must be the work of God, not mine.

The apostle Paul, knowing God does not condemn Timothy for his shortcomings (Romans 8:1), encourages and gives grace to him as they walk along the path of their lives together. Still, many Pauls are tempted to "fix" their Timothys because they believe they see an answer to their problems. Resisting this temptation is critical because that answer may not be God's answer. Often the fixing can be construed as condemnation or judgment. Paul's role in the process is to be a source of unconditional love, avoiding condemnation and judgment of Timothy's unrighteous behavior. If not, Paul could lose his status as a safe person for Timothy.

At the same time, Timothy does need accountability to mature in his walk with Christ. My focus is to encourage Timothy. Positive words of encouragement are an excellent motivator and I use them liberally. I expect the Holy Spirit and the Scriptures to take care of the conviction Timothy will need in his life regarding things not pleasing to God. I must resist the temptation to do the Holy Spirit's work. Otherwise I chance losing my role as an encourager and grace giver for Timothy.

One of the things I have had to do in the area of encouragement is learn to be a good listener. God has given us two ears and one mouth. We should keep this two-to-one ratio in mind. When working with Timothy, I need to ask questions and listen. Telling him what to do is a mistake that should be avoided; this works contrary to the discipling process. If he asks a question I will give him an answer. However, giving unsolicited advice is something I shouldn't engage in as it might frustrate him. Timothy needs accountability, but sometimes does not realize this need. My role is to pray for Timothy and ask how it is going for him in the areas where God is working. Conversely, in the areas God is not currently working, I encourage him to wait on the Lord's timing.

As change takes place in Timothy's life he begins to realize God is active in his life. God will reward his modified behavior, which is an answer to his and Paul's prayers. The changes God is making may not be obvious or even logical to our minds, but rest assured God has a plan and is working out the steps.

I have many experiences of seeing God at work. Sharing stories about these experiences with Timothy is the most effective way to give encouragement and extend grace to him. Jesus shared parables born out of His agrarian culture. Men relate well to stories out of the culture in which they live. Sharing personal, actual life experiences enables me to point out to Timothy the work God is doing in my life. This is a critical need because it helps Timothy to learn from my stories, to thank God, and be able to extend encouragement and grace to others.

Often Timothy is coming from a point in life where he has been crushed and is reaping what he has sown. As he becomes accountable, he will learn to live and experience the victorious, abundant life Christ promises. In the early stages of the discipleship process, Timothy has sown a lot of negative things and is still reaping the results. I have to keep encouraging him or he may be defeated by the negative attacks of the world and the evil one. As he begins to sow righteous thoughts, words and actions, the victorious life begins to emerge.

Life change comes as he gets into the Scriptures and develops a relationship with God through the Word. God uses His Word to point out where Timothy has gotten off the path of righteousness. He may be so far away from a life accountable to God when he begins the process that it takes a lot of grace and encouragement to keep him trusting God for the changes.

## Timothy's story

Experiencing God's grace through my Paul gave me a great sense of being cared for and loved, especially when I did not feel like my behavior warranted it. One of the greatest acts of grace and encouragement came at a time when, during a difficult time in our marriage, my wife and I were separated for several months. I had decided that while separated I would not date or get involved with another woman so that I could keep focused on my marriage. Because of my great neediness for attention and affection, however, I was caught off guard by a woman who began to show interest in a subtle way.

This woman happened to be married and I worked with her. Her being a married woman was, in the beginning, a major deterrent to my having any involvement with her. However, as time went on I allowed myself to be led astray by her crafty way of appealing to my neediness, and eventually she enticed me into an adulterous relationship. Proverbs 7:10-22 speaks of a woman of this kind: *"And there a woman met him, with the attire of a harlot, and a crafty heart. She was loud and rebellious; her feet would not stay at home. 'Come, let us take our fill of love until morning; let us delight ourselves with love. For my husband is not at home, he has gone on a long journey'; with her enticing speech she caused him to yield, with her flattering lips she seduced him. Immediately he went after her, as an ox goes to the slaughter or as a fool to the correction of the stocks."* That essentially described me.

So after choosing to become physically intimate with her, I was overwhelmed by the Holy Spirit's conviction. I went to my Paul to confess what I had done. I was fully expecting to be admonished for my behavior. However, after confiding my sins with my Paul, he shared that he too had been involved in an adulterous relationship in a previous marriage. Because of grace he had received from God in his situation, he was able to extend that same grace and understanding to me. There was no condemnation, judgment, lectures or finger-pointing. I had never experienced grace like this before.

He encouraged me to break off the relationship and move on, which I did. However, the emotional hooks were so deep into me that I returned to the relationship. At this point I was admonished by my Paul, and God gave me up to my own lustful desires. My Paul also let me go and gave me over to God.

Over the next year he would call me occasionally to see how I was doing. Because I was choosing to live in sin, I separated myself from my Paul and spiritual family because they represented the light, which I could not bear at this time.

After about a year, God revealed the truth about this woman from Proverbs 7:24-27: *"Now therefore, listen to me, my children; pay attention to the words of my mouth: do not let your heart turn aside to her ways, Do not stray into her paths; for she has cast down many wounded, and all who were slain by her were strong men. Her house is the way to hell, descending to the chambers of death."* That passage caught my attention.

True to this Proverb, I discovered there were other men she had wounded and lured into her house of destruction. It was revealed I was not the first man with whom she had committed adultery. There were two others before me. At this point I had my fill of my own lustful desires, which God had given me up to, and was finally ready to receive the truth from the Word about this relationship. When I succeeded in ending it, much relief followed.

I went back to my Paul to confess the wayward life I had been living. He once again received me with grace and joy, much as the father did with the prodigal son in Luke 15:11-24: *"But when he was still a great way off, his father saw him and had compassion, and ran and fell on his neck and kissed him. And the son said to him, 'Father, I have sinned against heaven and in your sight, and am no longer worthy to be called your son.' But the father said to his servants, 'Bring out the best robe and put it on him, and put a ring on his hand and sandals on his feet. And bring the fatted calf here and kill it, and let us eat and be merry; for this my son was dead and is alive again; he was lost and is found.' And they began to be merry."*

I was also graciously accepted back into my spiritual family. This whole experience of being handled with grace and patience during this time of my life has always been a great source of encouragement to me.

## Scripture references

1 Peter 5:5b-6; James 1:19; Galatians 6:7-8; John 10:10; 2 Timothy 3:16-17; Romans 8:1

· · · · · · · · · · · · · · · · · · · · · · · · · · · · · · · · · · · · · · · · · · · · · · · · · · · · · · · · · · · · · · · · · · · · · · · · · · · · ·

# Questions for reflection or discussion

· · · · · · · · · · · · · · · · · · · · · · · · · · · · · · · · · · · · · · · · · · · · · · · · · · · · · · · · · · · · · · · · · · · · · · · · · · · · ·

What are your comments on this chapter?



What has been your personal experience with this topic?



Any Scriptures or principles discussed in this chapter you need to apply in your life?

# 16.
# Scripture Memory

················································

*"How can a young man keep his way pure? By living according to your word. I have hidden your word in my heart that I might not sin against you."*
Psalm 119:9, 11

## Paul's perspective

As I walk through life, the enemy comes at me, seeking to discourage and tempt me, similar to how he did with Jesus in the wilderness (Matthew 4:1-11). Jesus dealt with Satan by refuting his lies, using clear references to God's truth from God's Word. The Scriptures are God's clear and direct communication to my heart and mind that will strengthen and encourage me as I live a life committed to following Christ. Through the conviction of the Holy Spirit my will is changed to align with God's will for my life. This change, however, is not me conforming by self-effort to His will or reforming myself. Rather it is a spiritual transformation empowered by the Holy Spirit.,

The disciplemaking process has demonstrated that men that do not memorize Scripture rarely go on to become disciplemaking Pauls. They merely experience the initial phases of the discipleship process. Those who do not stick with Scripture memorization struggle and eventually fade away. So as I meet with Timothy, I pray God will give him a lifelong hunger to engrave the Word on his heart so that he will be less likely to sin against the Lord. The Word is food that provides the spiritual energy needed for a man to finish the race and keep the faith.

Scripture memory with my Timothy is not a duty or one-time performance, but the way he and I will grow deeper in our relationship with each other and the Lord. Getting men started is often a baby step-like process. I begin by helping my Timothy succeed in getting one verse memorized and understood, working on that verse in our one-on-one time together, until he embraces it. Eighteen key verses that support eighteen of the topics Timothy and I will initially study in the *Operation Timothy* booklets* make up the first phase of his memory work. I encourage him to grow in his memory work by adding new verses. Memory verse packets from the Topical Memory System Life Issues material* that include 60 verses have been used by many of my Timothys as they continue to embed God's Word in their hearts.

*(Available through www.cbmc.com)

A Paul must be committed to fight the battle with his Timothy that comes as Satan provides opposition. Equipped with Scripture in his heart, a man can succeed in the process of maturing in the formation of Christ within him. Without the Scriptures, he is easy prey for Satan's tactics that paralyze him, render him useless, and ultimately take him out of the race.

## Timothy's story

As a new Timothy meeting with my Paul during *Operation Timothy*, I personally remember my Paul informing me it would be good to memorize a verse. I informed him I could not memorize anything. He replied that he thought I could. I explained to him that school assignments that required memorization always resulted in my having to take a zero and make the grade up somewhere else.

My Paul then asked for my telephone number. I gave it to him. Then he asked my address. I rattled it off. He said if I could recite those two things, he believed I could recite a verse. Yet I dug my heels in and continued to say no. He then instructed me to memorize 1 John 5:11-12 for the next meeting we had scheduled.

Though I did my lesson, I still did not memorize the verse. During our meeting, he asked me if I had memorized the verse. Being honest, I replied flatly, "I do not memorize."

"Okay, we will just memorize it now," he responded. This began a very painful thirty minutes of my life. We began memorizing a few words, then a sentence, and within a half hour I had my first verse.

As I walked out of that meeting I remember saying, "Gosh, I memorized my first verse." I had done it! To me it was such a miracle. My Paul believed enough in the importance of Scripture memorization and believed I needed it enough that he was willing to walk with me, even to the point of sitting beside me and going through the agonizing process of getting Scripture into my heart through my (hard) head.

From that day on I began memorizing other verses. Even today, so many years later, I still memorize new verses. This was the beginning of my seeing the value of Scripture memory.

When I am memorizing Scripture I have experienced God teaching me through one, two or three words in a verse that I had skipped over. Once, while memorizing Philippians 4:6-7, for some reason I was leaving out two words in the middle of the verse, "with thanksgiving." Every time I was checked on the verse, I would not include those two words. So I asked God why I was leaving the "with thanksgiving" out.

God graciously conveyed to me the reason was because I was not thankful. I asked Him to help me, and over time He created in me a heart that indeed was thankful. This was a wonderful gift from God. Up to that point I felt what I accomplished was a result of my own efforts. I had not seen my accomplishments as gifts from God. Now I realize that God gives me all things for which I am thankful. This was life-changing. I began to see God at work not just in the big things but also in many small things. I began to apply this realization over and over in my walk with God.

I remember hearing pastor/teacher Chuck Swindoll saying that of all of his spiritual disciplines, including quiet time and prayer, Scripture memory has had the greatest impact. This was a tremendous statement; I can say this is true for me as well.

Today, as a Paul, I ask God to give my Timothys a lifelong hunger for Scripture memory. In the beginning, Timothy and I may be locked in a battle over my strong belief in his need for Scripture memory and his struggle to do the hard work of memorization. If my Timothy goes on without developing this discipline he has won our battle, but in the long run he has lost the war.

Colorado businessman Bob Foster often has said he uses an acronym *ACQUIRED* when training men to memorize. This idea of acquiring a verse gave men clarity to the memorization process. The word ACQUIRED stands for:

(A) At one sitting
(C) Correctly
(Q) Quoting
(U) Unassisted
(I) Including
(R) References
(E) Eliminating
(D) Doubt

This is a neat way of saying that when you have acquired a verse, you now own that verse. And it has become yours. Then you can say the verse to someone else. Not many people get a hold of the Scriptures and memorize them. It's a team thing between me and my Timothy as I encourage and, at times, gently push him to acquire verses. This is something he and I can share the rest of our days.

## Scripture references

Psalm 119:9, 11; Matthew 4:1-11; Timothy 3:16-17; Romans 12:2; 2 Timothy 4:7; 1 John 5:11-12; Philippians 4:6-7

......................................................................................

## Questions for reflection or discussion
......................................................................................

What are your comments on this chapter?

What has been your personal experience with this topic?

Any Scriptures or principles discussed in this chapter you need to apply in your life?

# 17.
# Training
......................

*"So I will very gladly spend for you everything
I have and expend myself as well...."
2 Corinthians 12:15*

## Paul's perspective

A Paul trains his Timothy during the one-on-one discipleship process, but not as a result of mechanical and legalistic methodology. This
training happens over time in the fellowship of a Paul giving his life to
Timothy, where a Paul models the life of Christ in himself before Timothy's eyes. Learning to live this new life in Christ is caught – and not
taught – over time with no predetermined finish point. It is a process,
not a program or project. I am used by God to oversee Timothy's discipleship training. As a father oversees the training of his genetic children, equipping them to leave home and make their way in the world, I
train Timothy so he can disciple another man. In many cases Timothy
does not realize he is being trained because Paul has not made training
a focus of the relationship. Yet Timothy becomes trained because he sees
the fruit of Paul's life and he "imitates" it.

The discipleship training opportunity could last only a few minutes;
a simple, one-time encounter. Sometimes it's a lifetime process extending all the way to the grave. In the beginning, attaching to Timothy and
entering his world for a long period of time involves us being in close
geographical proximity. We meet often, usually weekly or biweekly as
schedules allow. When we begin our studies of the Word, he needs time
in between meetings to study and prepare for our next meeting.

Each meeting includes time for sharing our lives, praying for our
needs, and praying for the needs of others. Equally important is getting
into the study materials and letting God's Word impact our lives as we

review and discuss Scripture. Once our meetings get into this type of format, it will typically continue for a couple of years.

As Timothy's spiritual transformation begins to take place before my eyes, I am encouraged by God's visible work in this man. There will be areas of spiritual equipping that Timothy may struggle with that require special attention. The more common struggles include his testimony, Scripture memory, a life purpose statement, financial responsibility, relationship with his wife, and identifying a man to disciple. But these struggles are good. They are used in Timothy's life as a part of God's process for developing character, trust and hope.

A necessary part of His training process for Timothy is the suffering that tests his faith. Suffering is the wilderness experience a man will go through at some point in his life. After Jesus was baptized, He was led by the Spirit into the wilderness to be tempted by the Devil. Jesus quoted the Word to the Devil and his temptations were resisted. I assist Timothy in understanding that the enemy is tempting him to lose his faith – and that the Word is his defense. Using Jesus' example in the wilderness trains a man to go to the Word and rely on God's promises to defeat Satan's temptations.

After several years (between one to five years would be common), Timothy needs to begin detaching from me and decreasing his dependence on me. During the early years I have, at times, taken the place of God in his life. Not intentionally, of course, but initially he needs flesh and bone, a human being that he can see, talk to and hear. I model for him the lifestyle of looking to Jesus and the Father for security and companionship. Gradually he too will learn to look to God for all his needs to be met. By now he should be "drinking out of his own well," feeding himself with the basics of prayer, the Word, and fellowship.

During this time, I have been connecting him with other men involved in the one-on-one discipleship work, and he can begin to get involved in lifestyle evangelism. (The Lifestyle Evangelism chapter covers this in more detail). I have identified venues he is comfortable with that we can engage in with the other men, like golf, sporting events, tennis, fishing, concerts, and businessmen's lunches. This is a part of the life-on-life process I use to train Timothy to be effective with other men. We will attend movement retreats, outreaches, vacation weeks in the Texas hill country, and meetings where ministry training is conducted.

The men I am introducing him to will become a network of like-minded followers of Christ that will help meet some of his relationship needs. A functioning and ongoing network is necessary for Timothy to detach from me in a healthy way as part of the one-on-one discipleship process.

Detaching involves reducing the number and frequency of our regularly scheduled one-on-one meetings. We should be getting into the "living the ministry out before others" part of the process. I will be connecting with his friends and family members, and he with mine. These are some of the people we are trying to reach for Christ. Together we are actively carrying out the cultivation, sowing, harvesting, and discipling aspects of God's plan for the "ministry of reconciliation" with people in our sphere of influence.

The tension of knowing how to attach to men, along with the tension of how to detach from them, are part of Paul's struggle. There is no formula or guidebook to follow. I have a plan and keep looking to God to guide my steps while anticipating He is working all things out for Timothy's and my good. The attaching and detaching is a God thing as He draws men to me and moves them away from me. God is a jealous God, and He must have these men dependent on Him alone, not in another man.

Years ago I took a Red Cross class certifying me to teach swimming to young children. To qualify for the class we had to swim 440 yards nonstop just to get into the class. For most people this is a long, hard swimming test. When we finished the swim, our instructor took us to the steps in the shallow end of the pool. Young children first learn to swim by putting their face in the water and blowing bubbles. He told us we needed to put our face in the water and blow bubbles. So we all did. I felt a little silly doing this humbling elementary task, but the instructor made his point with me. If you want to be a teacher you must be trainable, because that is what teachers do, train people. In the JPT (Jesus, Paul, Timothy) process, trainable men that are willing to master the basics, such as Scripture memory, quiet time, accountability, prayer and finances, to name just five, usually go on to train and disciple others.

In meetings with Timothy, the subject of discipling another man will come up. Ideally, when he is ready, God will send a man he can give his life to as I have been doing with him. Training him in such a way that he will be able to disciple another man is a critical aspect of the JPT Process.

If Timothy is able to begin effectively discipling another man, the process of disciplemaking has been successfully accomplished.

Trainability is an aspect of Timothy's spiritual growth that makes or breaks him in the reproductive discipleship process. He can be faithful, available and teachable, yet unable to reproduce the process in another man because he is not trainable. The reasons he is not trainable are unique to each man. The battle over his struggles is within – between him and God. Often at the root of his struggle is not a lack of understanding, but a issue of the heart. Christ has a heart for the lost and for spiritual reproduction. If his intimacy with Christ is lacking, his heart's desire to do the will of Christ will be lacking.

When I am intimate with Christ, I love what He loves and want to have my priorities in line with His priorities. My role is to be there for Timothy and continue encouraging him to seek intimacy with Christ and to find a man to disciple.

## Timothy's story

In meetings with my Paul, he began praying for a man with whom I could meet. This subject came up after we had covered about 80 percent of the material in the *Operation Timothy* study guide. Finding a man was a difficult process for me because I did not know where to begin or how to start.

My Paul would bring it up every time we met, and we prayed for a man. When he asked if I had a man, I would make an excuse. "What are you so afraid of?" he asked. I told him I was not afraid but just did not know all that much. I felt I would be unprepared for meeting with another man. He said, "If any questions come up in your meeting, just write them down, call me, and I'll provide the answers." He also added that I needed to realize because of my studying with him, I was now in the top 10 percent of all the Christians in the world with regard to my knowledge of the Bible. Wow! This statement amazed me and gave me confidence to go ask someone to meet with me.

At that time in my life I was a tennis professional giving lessons to a psychologist. I shared with him that I had just finished going through a Bible study and needed to find someone to meet one-on-one with me. I asked him if he knew anything about the Bible. He said he did not. He was an excellent candidate for me because I wanted someone who did not know anything so that I could feel more knowledgeable. He agreed to meet with me at his home, a 22-mile drive from my place of business.

I was a busy businessman and had little spare time. I went to his home at 6:30 p.m. for our meeting. After a long trip to his home in traffic, I discovered his wife and three children were there but he was not. I waited for an hour and then left. I called my Paul on the way home and told him my experience, telling him I just did not have time for such inconveniences. "I am just too busy for this," I claimed.

He quizzed me, asking what I thought God was doing in this situation. "I have no idea," I responded. He quickly replied, "God is testing you, determining if you are a faithful man, enough so to reach another man and help him as I have helped you." I had not considered that as being the issue. So, at the encouragement of my Paul, I agreed to continue with this man.

After about six months of meeting with him, he said he would have to stop. He explained that if he decided to have a relationship with Jesus Christ he would have to change his business because it was contrary to his training. Before he was a psychologist he was an anesthesiologist. He had changed his career path because he just did not like anesthesiology, and he could not even consider changing his business a third time. So this relationship ended, with much seed planted into his heart, but my Paul was right there helping me find another man.

He helped me get started and stay the course. I have been discipling men for more than 30 years, and it was my Paul's encouragement and training that got me started and prompted me onward. I have done the same for a number of men over the last thirty years.

## Scripture references

1 Thessalonians 2:8; Proverbs 22:6; Psalm 90:10; Isaiah 43:4; Romans 5:3-5; Matthew 4:1-11; 2 Corinthians 5:18; Proverbs 16:9; Romans 8:28; Ex. 20:4-6; 2 Timothy 2:2: Luke 19:10; Luke 15:3-7: Matthew 28:19-20

. . . . . . . . . . . . . . . . . . . . . . . . . . . . . . . . . . . . . . . . . . . . . . . . . . . . . . . . . . . . . . . .
## *Questions for reflection or discussion*
. . . . . . . . . . . . . . . . . . . . . . . . . . . . . . . . . . . . . . . . . . . . . . . . . . . . . . . . . . . . . . . .

What are your comments on this chapter?

What has been your personal experience with this topic?

Any Scriptures or principles discussed in this chapter you need to apply in your life?

# 18.
# Disputable Matters

······························

*"If you do anything you believe is not right, you are sinning."*
Romans 14:23b (New Living Translation)

### Paul's perspective

The history of Christianity is littered with breakups and even wars over disputable Biblical matters. The reason there are so many different Christian denominations can be traced to arguments sufficient enough to cause division over disputable matters.

Our spiritual enemy looks for opportunities to use disputable matters to create chaos and separate Timothy and me. Examining which denominations have it right and which do not seems like one of Satan's favorite diversions. The relationship that has developed over time between Timothy and me must allow him the freedom to explore his own understanding of the Scriptures. Timothy's beliefs about disputable matters may be rooted in his religious background or family traditions. Breaking free from one's past involves looking afresh at the Word of God, thus allowing the Holy Spirit to bring conviction as to what God is saying. I find this is the best way to deal with the confusion and doubt that disputable matters can create.

Embracing incorrect doctrine usually involves accompanying values and behaviors. Continued allegiance, like bad habits, is more visible with the backdrop of God's truth. Time and ongoing fellowship between Timothy and me should eventually expose and clarify God's truth for us both. I have my own convictions about most disputable matters, but allowing them to separate and/or interfere with our relationship is not acceptable to me.

One common area of disputable matters consists of the "dos and don'ts." It is here where the individual, as he is responsible to God, wrestles with lifestyle and weighs each matter in his own conscience, an essential part of individual spiritual growth. Actually God is the decision-maker about dos and don'ts - not what other people think or say about the matter. Convictions I have about drinking, smoking, church, R-rated movies and other such matters should come from the Lord's conviction as I walk with Him and He directs through knowledge of Scripture.

I prefer to let the Timothy struggle with disputable matters as we walk through the Word, allowing the prompting of the Holy Spirit to convict and direct his understanding. I will, however, gladly point him to various Scripture references that can help as he wrestles with the disputable matter.

It is best, whenever disputable matters arise, to briefly address them, move on, regroup, and then refocus on the basics for what it means to be a follower of Christ. These include: placing Christ at the center of my life; devotion to prayer; being attentive in Scripture reading; fellowship; being a witness; obedience to Christ, and yes, allowing God to break me whenever and in whatever ways change is necessary. I am always blessed when I redirect Timothy and myself back to the basics. Our relationship quickly restores itself to the sweetness of the Christ-centered fellowship that I have come to enjoy and long for.

### Timothy's story

As a young believer, I had a habit of stopping at a local restaurant and bar after work and meeting up with friends. As I began studying the Scriptures I realized that after a few beers I had a much greater appreciation for the ladies at the bar. I lacked the self-control encouraged by Scripture. One evening my wife was with me and noticed this habit, so she began discussing it with me. This became a problem in our relationship because it conflicted with her need for security. She felt very insecure when I was looking at other women.

My Paul continued to impart the Scriptures, and the Holy Spirit began working with me in this area. Little by little I realized that even though there was no reason I could not go into a bar, it was best for me either not to go at all or to limit my drinking to a beer or two. The Lord graciously led me to develop self-control, both with alcohol and with my eyes.

## *Scripture references*

Romans 14:23b; Ephesians 5:3; Hebrews 10:24-25; Galatians 5:22-23

. . . . . . . . . . . . . . . . . . . . . . . . . . . . . . . . . . . . . . . . . . . . . . . . . . . . . . . . . . . . . . . . .

# *Questions for reflection or discussion*

. . . . . . . . . . . . . . . . . . . . . . . . . . . . . . . . . . . . . . . . . . . . . . . . . . . . . . . . . . . . . . . . .

What are your comments on this chapter?

What has been your personal experience with this topic?

Any Scriptures or principles discussed in this chapter you need to apply in your life?

# 19.
# Learning Not to Teach

......................................................

*"One day Jesus was praying in a certain place. When he*
*finished, one of his disciples said to him, 'Lord, teach us to pray,*
*just as John taught his disciples." He said to them, 'When you*
*pray, say: Father, hallowed be your name, your Kingdom come.'"*
*Luke 11:1-2*

## *Paul's perspective*

In the Scriptures, Jesus often called the disciples to be with Him, so
the disciples were constantly watching His life. On one occasion they
observed Jesus praying and asked Him to teach them to pray. He prayed
what is commonly referred to as "the Lord's Prayer" with them, giving an
example for them to follow. Later, He sent them out ahead to the places
where He was about to go so they could do what they had seen Him do.

The apostle Paul also wrote to his followers, encouraging them to
imitate the things they had seen him do. The things they had heard him
say, he exhorted them to entrust to reliable men who could pass them on
to other trustworthy men.

Learning not to teach sounds strange because many Christians see
discipleship and teaching as one and the same. However, I do not view
them that way. A person gifted as a teacher has the ability to recognize
truths from the Scriptures and teach them in an understandable way. A
Paul having the gift of teaching will feel the need to present truth to his
Timothy by teaching a lesson. An experienced discipler, however, has
learned that helping a man discover the truth as he examines the Scriptures is the desirable result of discipling. Sharing his discoveries with me
serves to confirm them and encourages Timothy to feed himself with
Biblical truth. Effective study of the Scriptures, with prayer and along
with conviction by the Holy Spirit, leads Timothy to God's truth.

Teachers are usually someone you meet in a classroom. Churches are filled with teachers. Students sit in classroom sessions, being fed information by teachers. When they leave the classroom setting, however, typically no behavioral change has taken place. That is because students don't see the lesson in action. It's merely theory. The student can see little change without seeing the lesson lived out in someone's life. Classroom teaching has its place, but it is not a big part of the one-on-one discipleship process.

The teaching I do comes from modeling a commitment of obedience to Jesus' commandments. I can lecture all I want on obedience and still manage to blow the whole lesson with one display of ungodly behavior, which I have done. The path I try to take, rather than lecturing, is sharing my struggles and communicating to Timothy that only Jesus can live out the Christian life in me.

As a discipler, I must strive *not* to teach. Instead, I concentrate on the fact that the best learning comes out of observing the life of an individual, not from a classroom lecture. Life change comes out of observing a life worth looking at and listening to the personal perspectives of the person being observed. Most of the behavior change results from seeing life modeled out, which makes people curious. Creating curiosity without telling and giving the answers is really the essence of *learning not to teach.*

A professional man I was discipling shared with me how busy, anxious and chaotic his life had become. He observed that I seemed relaxed, having plenty of time to meet with him whenever he could squeeze me in. I shared with him that twenty years earlier, searching for peace and order in my life, I had committed to a 25-hour workweek. That required trusting God to provide the necessary income, which He had done since then very satisfactorily. My Timothy shook his head and doubted that plan could ever work for him. Nothing more was said; he just kept observing me. Two years later, growing more relaxed as he followed my lead, he instituted a four-day workweek for himself and began committing some of his free time to recreation, ordering his life, and praying for a man to meet with.

Once Timothy discovers a truth in the Scriptures, I need to let him determine its application. A truth discovered becomes a life-changing truth when Timothy makes application and transformation comes by the Holy Spirit.

From my perspective, discipleship is five percent teaching and 95 percent relationship building. My focus is on building a relationship with Timothy and witnessing his emerging, growing relationship with God. I am to share the truth of God to Timothy in the context of my life. Along the way, my hope is to impact people as a man who is living the life of Christ for others to see, rather than teaching in a classroom, realizing that this is how Jesus and Paul did it. A wise old man once wrote, "I would rather see a sermon than hear one any day. I would rather one would walk with me than merely point the way." Living life before others is the essence of learning not to teach people.

## Timothy's story

Recently I was meeting with my Timothy and we were reviewing a memory verse, 1 Peter 5:8-9: *"Be self-controlled and alert. Your enemy the devil prowls around like a roaring lion looking for someone to devour. Resist him, standing firm in the faith, because you know that your brothers throughout the world are undergoing the same kind of sufferings."* Instead of telling my Timothy what I thought the verse meant, I asked him what he thought about it. His first thought was that the enemy is fierce and powerful and looking to kill, steal, and destroy the life of a Christian.

In regard to verse 9, we looked at how differently Eve and Jesus Christ handled the temptations of the lust of flesh, lust of the eyes, and pride of life as they were tempted by the enemy in these three areas. From Timothy's perspective, Eve did not resist the enemy. Instead, she entertained and chewed on the temptations, eventually giving in to them and allowing the enemy to kill, steal and destroy her relationship with God. On the other hand, Christ did not blink an eye, but quickly and decisively confronted the enemy with the truth – the Word of God – and the enemy eventually fled. Christ went on the offensive, never giving the enemy an opportunity to establish a foothold as Eve had done.

My Timothy determined that Christ resisted the enemy and stood firm in His faith, but Eve failed, both in resisting and failing to stand firm in her faith in God. Her faith was in herself, not God. My Timothy also found encouragement and took comfort in understanding that other brothers around the world suffer the same things that he does. By asking for and welcoming his thoughts, I am not the focus, which leaves him to work through the Scriptures with God and be taught by Him – and not me.

### Scripture references

Luke 11:1-2; 1 Corinthians 4:15a (NLT); Mark 3:14; Luke 10:1; Philippians 4:9; 2 Timothy 2:2; Hebrews 13:5; Deuteronomy 6:7; 1 Peter 5:8-9; Genesis 3:1-8

..............................................................................

## Questions for reflection or discussion
..............................................................................

What are your comments on this chapter?

What has been your personal experience with this topic?

Any Scriptures or principles discussed in this chapter you need to apply in your life?

# 20.
# A Process

..........................

*"By the grace God has given me, I laid a foundation as an expert builder, and someone else is building on it. But each one should be careful how he builds. For no one can lay any foundation other than the one already laid, which is Jesus Christ."*
1 Corinthians 3:10-11

## Paul's perspective

My challenge as a Paul is to meet Timothy where he is, laying down the foundation of Christ, and staying one step ahead of him as he grows. If I stay just one step ahead I become his friend; if I get two steps ahead I may become his foe. By getting alongside him with small challenges that do not discourage him, we keep the process moving as he grows, one baby step at a time.

Building a man is not like the orderly project of building a house where the builder will follow a straight-forward process: (a) clear the lot, (b) pour the slab, (c) frame the structure, (d) build the rooms, (e) finish the interior, etc. I have heard it said that a typical house is made up of 48,000 separate parts. I believe a complex human would far exceed that number, and working with them is not nearly as neat or predictable as constructing a house. So I leave the process of building a person of Christ-like character to God.

When I begin the discipleship process with a man, discovering what is going on with him is critical to the relationship. Often there is a lot of turmoil in his life. I must be transparent with Timothy so he feels safe in opening up with me about the areas of struggle in his life. God may be working in his marriage, parenting, work, finances, sex life, family of origin issues, unresolved conflicts with other people, Biblical disciplines, and his health. These things cannot be viewed from a linear perspective, but from the perspective of where God may be working in his life. As Timothy and I meet, pray, and get into the Word, God will enter the process, delivering revelations that will impact both of us in a supernatural way.

Discipling Timothy is not a linear process. I use the word *linear* to indicate an orderly process that proceeds from beginning to end, A to Z, step by step. Timothy lives in a global world full of disorder and chaos that will interrupt and sidetrack his spiritual growth. The spiritual maturity process has necessary foundational steps such as developing a prayer life, knowledge of the Word, fellowship, witnessing, salvation, sanctification, and other spiritual disciplines. These development areas are ongoing in a chaotic world. Notice I use the word *process,* not program or project. Again, a program or project has an orderly, predetermined start and a finish. Timothy is not a project of mine. God is in the business to building and changing men, not me. I'm just an instrument in that process.

Another way of looking at Timothy's growth is comparing it to that of a baby. An infant is unable to eat solid food until his teeth start coming in, usually from six to nine months. Just as we feed babies only milk or special formula, Timothy must be fed simple basics until he develops the maturity to digest more complex spiritual food. I must be careful not to give him assignments beyond where he is spiritually, but to give him simple things he can digest.

Most businessmen don't read much, limiting that activity to the newspaper, something on the computer screen, or maybe a book on golf – if it is short. So even reading the Bible may be a new endeavor for them. The study of Scriptures, with all the new words and terms, can be overwhelming because their minds are filled with a lot of junk. The purging of this junk moves slowly and I am careful to let it occur as a natural process rather than forcing its progress. I keep in mind first and foremost that God is building the men and doing so in a non-linear fashion, as life just comes at them and often seems to us without rhyme or reason.

Being a Paul for men who, by their nature, are systematic, literal, structured, methodical-type individuals, is often a struggle. Typically these are people who live in a world of linear projects with well-defined beginnings and endings. These men struggle with discipleship because it is not methodical. It often takes place in what seems like conceptual chaos. As Pauls meet with their Timothys and find that they do not conform to the "rules," often they are not able to accept their lack of structure. The discipleship process can become stymied because Paul establishes rules or requirements he believes will move a man through the process in the same manner God moved him. Helping high-structure types understand God is at work in an unstructured way (at least from our perspective) is my role. Learning to meet and accept Timothy where he is at the moment will allow him to grow in grace, and increase the likelihood of him becoming a reproducer.

When Timothy has matured to the point he has found a man to disciple and takes on the role of a Paul, I become a sounding board for his discipling process with this new man. Victory in this process will not take place by following a set of linear rules. Instead it will be a process of God building a man in a way that will at times make no logical sense to the finite human mind. Walking with my Timothy through the process is a role I must play, like a spiritual grandfather to the new man. I am there praying, offering encouragement to both of them, but not taking the primary role with the new Timothy.

Encouraging my Timothy to become a good listener with his Timothy is critical. God could be working in any given area, and by listening and identifying the area, he can begin to pray and encourage his man. By helping him move through the area God is working on, rather than trying to keep him focused on a set of rules, a God-engineered transformation will begin to take place.

My relationship with Timothy, as his spiritual parent, spiritual father or peer, may last a lifetime – mine and his. The process is about the relationship between Jesus, Paul and Timothy (JPT). The spiritual maturity of a man is not a concrete process, demanding that Timothy follow a set of rules that ensure his maturity. Learning to live humbly, understanding that Christ living through us is the only measure of true change, enables us to live the life that will glorify God.

## Timothy's story

I accepted Christ as my Savior in mid-life after experiencing a lot of pain and suffering. I was a spiritual blank page with little formal Christian knowledge and training. My conversion came about because I discovered, while reading the Gospels, Jesus' offer to me of a new way of life. The truth of my sin, guilt, and need for forgiveness jumped off the pages of the Gospel of John, chapter 3, and led me to a commitment to Christ.

I was hungry and found the program at a local church stimulating and informative. It was like going back to college, sitting in lectures and absorbing lots of information. A couple of years of this and I had become a lukewarm believer, having an abundance of Christian information but not knowing what to do with it. My personal life was another matter. It was characterized by chaos, disorganization, and disorientation, and filled with a wide assortment of problems.

I met a man who introduced me to the discipleship process but treated it more like a program. He spent six months with me as we reviewed the basics of the Christian faith. He then "graduated me." I felt better educated but still confused about how to effectively live out my faith. About this time I met my Paul, and he began to build into my life. With him it was not about obtaining knowledge as the first order. Instead, it was about our relationship and me feeding off his experience, knowledge and wisdom. His perspective often was 180 degrees from my own. I would debate him and he graciously yielded to my immature, worldly wisdom. Later I would recognize my foolishness and his wisdom.

The path of my life, its events and challenges, determined the lessons I was learning as I walked with my Paul. We searched the Scriptures, prayed and looked to God for answers. We have been walking together for a couple of decades, and my heart leaps with joy when we meet. It's the joy of knowing that God is going to be with us and speak to me through him. It's not an orderly, linear process. It's living day by day, taking the cards God deals, and playing out the hands according to the rules. There is nothing boring about this life of watching God at work in our lives and the lives of those we are connected with and bonded to in Christ.

### Scripture references

Corinthians 3:10-11; Romans 16:25; James 1:19; Romans 12:1-2; James 4:10; John 3:1-36; Revelation 3:16

..................................................................

## *Questions for reflection or discussion*

..................................................................

What are your comments on this chapter?

What has been your personal experience with this topic?

Any Scriptures or principles discussed in this chapter you need to apply in your life?

# 21.
# Team

············

*"After this the Lord appointed seventy-two others and sent
them two by two  ahead of him to every town and
place where he was about to go."*
*Luke 10:1*

## *Paul's perspective*

God accomplished a great deal using teams of humble men. Jesus
built a team, the disciples, and left the mission of imparting the Gospel message to that team. They were instructed to carry it forward to
following generations who would do the same. Effective teamwork is
learned when modeled in the environment of working with others on
a team. Teamwork is a necessary challenge for prideful men; it requires
the desire and willingness to die to their own desires and grow in Christ's
likeness. The nature of an effective team is based on the team member's
*commitment to Christ, commitment to the Gospel,* and *commitment to one
another.*

Members of a team may have to die to their own opinions and learn
to listen to God and other team members. To this end, pride can be a
formidable obstacle. Prideful men tend to think they know the best way.
As for prideful leaders, they often think other team members are there to
carry out their agenda. It is difficult for us as prideful men to die to our
own ways and honor others as being more important than ourselves. A
team member has to consider other members of the team as very important parts of the team as a whole. It is hard for prideful men to listen,
not just hear, because we think we know the way to resolve everything.
It is easy for us to become angry when our way was not the choice of the
other team members.

But working out our differences is one of the key issues in teamwork, so matters of pride must be cast aside. If it is time for us to yield to another's way, then we must fully cooperate and join the others in what the team is doing.

I have spent a number of years in Houston, Texas and have discipled a number of men. It has become natural for me to team up with these men to co-labor in the city's marketplace ministry. I believe teamwork is the Lord's way for getting His work accomplished, and a healthy approach for a movement that wins and disciples men in the marketplace. Sometimes dealing with team members can be a challenge and requires more time than if I were to just do something on my own. However, experience has taught me the "Lone Ranger" person is far less effective than a team. Put another way, the sum of the team's work can be (and usually is) greater than the results of individuals working independently of one another.

The fruit I labor for most passionately is found at the one-on-one level in the JPT (Jesus, Paul, Timothy) process. To accomplish this, my wife and I are a team, and my Timothy and I are a team. We and other core members of our movement team up to get things done most effectively, efficiently and fruitfully.

Whenever undertaking an event or project, one rule I steadfastly adhere to is I must have a team in place; otherwise I will not do it. My ministry is a team ministry.

Good teams (built with men who have been discipled in the movement) working together for long periods of time will experience five different leadership aptitudes that emerge among team members. Identification of these aptitudes is critical for developing and maintaining an effective team.

First there is the **Directive Leader**, someone that is charismatic, energizes people and develops the team objectives. Secondly, the **Strategic Leader**, one who gathers information to evaluate team options, is objective in his judgment and creative. The third aptitude is the **Team Building Leader**, someone who brings people together. This individual is most popular and spontaneous.

Fourth is the **Operational Leader**. He is management-styled in nature, develops systems, is good with details, and keeps a low profile. I'm thankful to author George Barna, from whom I learned these four aptitudes. I add to this list a fifth aptitude, that of overseer. The **Overseer Leader** of the team is a person who takes the role of a spiritual father; this person is mature and may be a patriarch or one in the making. He, like a parent with his children, recognizes the uniqueness of each individual on the team, treating them accordingly. He brings wisdom and maturity to the team process. In addition, he will also possess one of the four other leadership aptitudes and, to some degree, will have developed skills in the other three.

Effective teams develop the ability to get into *true community*. The relationships I form within these teams encourages me to faithfully stay the course. The community-building process is as follows: we start in *"pseudo-community,"* advance to *chaos,* and then enter *emptiness.* Out of emptiness we choose to set aside our differences, getting into *true community* and working with each other as a team. (For more details, the chapter on True Community and Appendix III cover the process of developing true community found in healthy and effective teams.)

As I meet with Timothy in our initial studies of the Bible, I invite him to participate in social events that are outreaches to secular people. This is the beginning of modeling for Timothy my involvement with people I am befriending. Often these occasions are at my house. Through such activities I am implanting the idea that he and I are a team of two, seeking to connect with awakening souls. Depending on Timothy's lifestyle, we may utilize his social life to do the same with people he knows. His network opens up new opportunities for evangelism and discipleship.

Teaming with my Timothys has trained them in the concepts and principles of team, community, and movements. These trained men, along with others they influence, have taken the principles learned and incorporated them into many things God is doing. The movement is not trying to control this synergy; rather it focuses on letting God take it wherever He wants it to go. Therefore, men working as teams have spread throughout their spheres of influence, becoming a God-centered crew free to go wherever the Spirit of God moves.

## Timothy's story

My background includes eight years as an athletic coach in the public school system. I was assigned three sports to coach each school year. The task of building 24 different teams during my coaching career led me to believe I knew quite a lot about team building. Also, I had been a member of at least that many teams as an athlete in public school and college. Because of my background with teams it was natural, when I became a follower of Christ at age 40, to discover ways to team up with others who shared my desire to communicate the "good news" of the Gospel.

What I found in organized religion was more of a corporate business model, one that talked "team" but did not function as healthy teams should. These organizations usually had a board of directors and levels of management that ran the organization just as any typical business operated, trying to make a profit. My eight years of working in the institutional public school system had confirmed I was not a person that functioned well in a corporate-type environment.

I left coaching, entered the business world and became involved in a businessman's ministry organized along the lines of a business as I described above. Within this organization I was finding useful tools, training and relationships with like-minded men. The organization, for the most part, allowed me to carry out my one-on-one discipleship without a lot of interference from the organizational structure.

My Paul, the local leader of the organization, began sharing with me his feelings that the model used by the organization was not the Biblical model of the movement that had spread the Gospel since the time of Jesus 2,000 years ago. He and I, along with two other like-minded men, began meeting and discussing the idea of becoming a different kind of ministry, a movement. It took several years of assessing how the ministry was functioning like organizations, compared to operating like a movement. As we met informally, a team mentality developed around our commitment to each other, the Gospel and Jesus Christ. This team bond grew stronger and our wives came aboard as supportive members of the team. This group holds no official position in the organizational structure of the ministry. It is the core of the movement's leadership and effective in developing strategy for the ministry.

Gradually, leadership and direction developed out of this team. The highly structured, organizational elements of the ministry were dismantled and replaced by healthy movement ministry elements. The movement began to spread like the wind, without a defined direction – but rather wherever God took it. The insiders realized they were empowered to step out and lead their own personal one-on-one ministries without a controlling organizational structure.

This team of four men and our wives has been endeavoring to lead by developing strategy behind the scenes for about ten years. We are watching the movement spread expansively in our city and other cities around the world. It is being broadcast by movement insiders as it naturally flows out of their JPT relationships in to other lives.

### Scripture references

Luke 10:1; Philippians 2:4; Matthew 28:19-20; Ephesians 4:4-6; 1 Peter 4:10

......................................................................
## Questions for reflection or discussion
......................................................................

What are your comments on this chapter?

What has been your personal experience with this topic?

Any Scriptures or principles discussed in this chapter you need to apply in your life?

# 22.
# Sending

......................

*"But you will receive power when the Holy Spirit comes on you;
and you will be my witnesses in Jerusalem, and in all Judea
and Samaria, and to the ends of the earth."*
*Acts 1:8*

### Paul's perspective

The JPT (Jesus, Paul, Timothy) movement is spread by disciplemakers who are sent by God to be "insiders." As insiders they befriend people, eventually leading them to Christ and discipling them. This usually will not happen quickly, but if it is God's work He will empower it and it will take place in His perfect timing.

As the number of Pauls increases, it is a given that some of them will get involved in the process I call "sending": By sending I am talking about a Paul or Timothy taking the JPT process to new men in new locations (neighborhoods, workplaces, other parts of the city, etc.).

The men I disciple are usually businessmen who may move around from job to job. Today, men under 40 tend to change jobs every three to five years. With each move they will interface with new men who might be Timothy candidates. A Paul's business moves may cause him to relocate to a new neighborhood, another city, state or country. Wherever he goes he is being sent by God, his spiritual family and the movement to serve as a disciplemaker in his new environment.

Once a Paul gets established in a new location, he begins the process of finding men he can disciple. His ministry will be the Timothys before whom he models the ministry. These men, along with the Paul, will make up a new team of movement insiders. Out of these discipled men God will bring about the generational multiplication of disciplemakers.

All of the men in the movement are insiders in the sense that they are in the Kingdom of God, have a genuine, personal relationship with Jesus Christ, and demonstrate a heart for one-on-one discipleship. Secondly, these men are now insiders in a new mini-culture and can begin to build relationships with those in the new environment. It is critical that the insider leaves all of his outward expressions of religion at home when he enters this new environment. He must keep his religious training and traditions under the radar. Otherwise he can quickly brand himself as "one of those holy Joe guys" and lose his opportunity to befriend non-believers in his new environment. Rather than proselyte the people, he must befriend them and remain focused on showing kindness to them. This behavior is attractive to others and comes out of his relationship with Christ. It will create curiosity about why he is so different.

God also sends men from other cities that have been discipled and may already be Pauls. These men become part of the local movement and spiritual family as they co-labor with us.

The few men who are called and desire to be in the full-time ministry are sent by the movement to cities having existing ministries that can raise their financial support. This is rare, however, because the vast majority of sending occurs with businessmen who produce their income – through so-called "secular" employment – to support their ministries.

The movement spreads randomly and spontaneously as men naturally move about in the marketplace. The movement looks to see where God has placed the Pauls and comes alongside them in support of their ministry. Unlike an organization that would undertake a formalized plan, this sending occurs unplanned, as God chooses and as He directs the places where men move, work and live.

## Timothy's story

The core group of our movement has been actively involved in overseeing and supporting sent men. The following three brief stories are about men who have been discipled in our local movement and then sent by God to establish their own ministries in other towns and cities:

**Timothy #1** came out of the world with an interesting background. He had lived a wild lifestyle in college and that continued after entering the working world. Then he got religious and married a preacher's daughter. Four kids later he submitted to one-on-one discipleship and his life was forever changed. With his spiritual maturity came a calling on his life to do the same with other men. He was called into full-time vocational ministry by an existing men's group in another city and has been there for more than ten years.

In the beginning, he focused on organizational aspects of ministry, developing events useful to men of the movement. After five years, however, he switched his focus to discipling men, realizing the disciples need to come first, before the events. The multiplication process of generational reproduction is progressing in his city. He has many men in various stages of the JPT process and as a result, many years of fruit bearing should follow.

**Timothy #2** came out of the institutional church in our city with a heart for reaching the lost. After submitting to the one-on-one discipleship process, he began reaching out to men in the culture at his work and in his neighborhood. The ministry work was so rewarding, he decided to leave his lucrative law practice and pursue other less stressful career options.

Several years of struggling led him and his wife to relocate to the city where they had gone to college. He went back into the legal profession, but this time as an associate and not as owner of his own firm. The new lifestyle gave him the freedom to focus on discipling men one-on-one. Over a period of several years, he has discipled a number of men in this new city. Today he has three faithful, available men who have teamed with him and are engaged with God in the process of what He is doing in their city. Recently, God sent another equipped man from our city to his city. This man has a supportive wife and he is joining their team. The movement is growing out of the JPT process and will be establishing local events that serve the ministry needs of this core group.

**Timothy #3** came to our movement when he and his family attended a family vacation week during the annual ministry event at a Texas hill country resort, Mo Ranch. During the week this businessman met some men that had such a profound impact on him, he wanted to know more about what they were doing.

Upon our return home, I called him and we began meeting together. As a new convert, he was hungry for the Word and proved to be a FAT (faithful, available and teachable) man. Once equipped in the one-on-one discipleship process, he found his own Timothy with whom to meet.

Within a few years he had several Timothys. He lives in a town that is about a 45-minute drive from the downtown area of our city. He and his wife were able to integrate into the movement's core group and spiritual family. There were a couple of discipled men in his town and he teamed with them, establishing a ministry.

He has been able to use the events and ministry forms that are already established in our city because of the close proximity of his town. Over a period of ten years he has taken ownership of the JPT movement in his town and has a clear vision for expanding the Kingdom in his local culture. By teaming with his wife and his Timothys, he is winning the lost and making disciples where he lives and works.

## Scripture references

Acts 1:8; 1 Corinthians 9:19-22; 2 Corinthians 2:15-16; Isaiah 60:22; 1 Corinthians 7:24; Matthew 28:19-20

...............................................................................

## Questions for reflection or discussion

...............................................................................

What are your comments on this chapter?

What has been your personal experience with this topic?

Any Scriptures or principles discussed in this chapter you need to apply in your life?

# 23.
# Retirement or Patriarch

·········································································

*"Moreover, when God gives any man wealth and possessions, and enables him to enjoy them, to accept his lot and be happy in his work – this is a gift of God. He seldom reflects on the days of his life, because God keeps him occupied with gladness of heart."*
*Ecclesiastes 5:19-20*

## *Paul's perspective*

My dad was a corporate man with a good pension who retired at age 65 and died at 93. He spent his retirement years entertaining himself with activities such as TV, watching the birds at the birdfeeder in his backyard, and driving to the convenience store to buy lottery tickets. His retirement did not appeal to me, so I never planned to retire. But we live during a time that encourages people to prepare for retirement even as they are entering the workforce. It is not uncommon to hear people still in their 20's preparing for and looking forward to the day they can retire. It seems that every fourth TV commercial is pushing some investment opportunity that will set people up for retirement in some picturesque location with perfect weather conditions.

My approach is different: I encourage Timothy to prepare for the future by spending less than he makes and learning to give. If he consistently spends less than he makes and saves the surplus, he should reach a point where cutting back or stepping out of his business career is an option. I do not find the concept of retirement in the Scriptures at all, except for Levitical priests, and even then they were charged with overseeing younger priests. The wise king Solomon said that a happy man is one that has work all the days of his life. Most of the businessmen I discipled will be working for a living in the marketplace for 30-40 years or more.

Often men never reach retirement because of burnout from the so-called rat race, or they die before reaching retirement age. They wear so many hats with the kids, the wife, the house, and life's problems, and everything else that is going on in this fast-paced culture in which we live. Men feeling a need for rest begin to think, "Someday I will retire, get a motor home, travel, and play golf, fish and recover from my life of toil and trouble." Too many men never make it to "someday" because they work themselves to death. They abuse their health with excesses in the areas of work, food, alcohol, and drugs, medicating their frustrations with a pressure-packed life.

Men need to take breaks throughout their career to avoid consequences of the burnout from lifestyles they are living. If men don't do this, they fry their brains and have nothing left at the end. Statistics show men often die within five to seven years after retiring. This doesn't seem like much time to reap the rewards of laboring three to five decades in the marketplace.

I encourage Timothy to begin thinking about a change of focus as he ages. Rather than preparing for traditional retirement, they can prepare to become a patriarch. The role of patriarch could give them a rewarding use of their lives as they cut back on their workdays or anticipate leaving their occupations. I model for Timothy the role of a patriarch, giving him a vision that "someday" his life can be ordered. This order – this well-conceived plan and purpose – will give him the margin necessary to live to be 70 or 80 years old, able to help other men, and oversee both his extended biological and spiritual families.

When Timothy becomes a Paul and begins discipling men for an extended time period, typically 20 years or more, he will have laid the foundation for becoming a patriarch. During these years he will put aside boyish behaviors, maturing as a man with a focused, ordered life. Although he has been meeting with men, a lot of his energy has been spent on taking care of his job and biological (or genetic) family.

After a couple of decades, Timothy (who by now has matured into a Paul), may have five to ten Timothys of his own that are Pauls or in the process of becoming a Paul. These men are in need of a patriarch that is devoting his life to his extended spiritual and genetic family. The patriarch is the backbone, cornerstone, anchor, point-guard, and linchpin of the family. He is the spiritual father for this family of men devoted to the JPT process of making disciples.

Due to his devotion over the years to his Timothys, the patriarch is respected for his wisdom, vision, creativity, credibility and integrity. His mindset is focused on both the process and relationship-building. His commitment is steadfast, he exhibits the freedom one can have in Christ, freely demonstrates grace, and is fully committed to his extended family.

Retirement for the patriarch is not an option with respect to those he has discipled and their extended family. If they are to make it through the jungle of this world intact, they will need a patriarchal spiritual father to guide them with his mature wisdom, creativity and insight. When the patriarch dies, he is not replaceable. He is one of a kind, yet his impact will be felt for generations.

If a man runs the race properly by taking appropriate pauses in his life to avoid burnout, one day he will wake up and discover he has become a patriarch. From my perspective, thinking that traditional retirement is Utopia is an ill-conceived, non-Biblical idea. God's plan for men is to become patriarchs, devoting the latter part of their lives to their extended families, and then going home to be with God.

*(Note: Not much has been written about the role of the patriarch in today's culture. However, "The Mature Man Becoming a Man of Impact" by David DeWitt is an excellent resource book if you want to know more about how to become one.)*

### Timothy's story

When I met my future wife she introduced me to a 70-year-old man who had been like a father to her. She had been in his home many times; at one time, in fact, it had looked like she would marry his son. Once she and I planned to marry, she asked him if he would perform the ceremony. He later became my Paul.

For our pre-marriage counseling he began meeting with us and we started talking about our differences. This made me feel like this man was really interested in me. No older man, including my father, had ever taken such an interest in me. I asked my fiancée what he did and who he was. She explained that he helped men with their spiritual life. I never realized there was such a thing as men who helped other men spiritually.

At my insistence she asked him if he would help me and spend a little time together with me.

Eventually we got into one-on-one discipleship and I began to see my life and the Scriptures coming together. I had never seen this before, but I witnessed scriptural principles actually working in real life. He invited me into his home and I observed how he and his wife functioned together. I had never seen a real-life marriage that was working. But as I looked at my Paul's marriage, I began to have hope that my new wife and I could have a marriage like theirs. It seemed so simple and made sense, yet it was profound. At the heart of their relationship, they really cared for each other.

As I looked at them and the Scriptures, it was like I had found a treasure. He would explain things to me and I was beginning to see how it all could work. Before, I had viewed the Bible was rote material with little or no practical relevance, and felt no connection with it or any desire to be involved. However, for my Paul the Bible was exciting and intriguing. It was like he had been to a really good movie. The Scriptures began to come alive for me. He was not teaching – he was simply imparting to me how the Scriptures had worked in his life and how its truths would work in my life.

After we spent some time together, I knew what my Paul was doing was something I wanted to do with my life. I did not know how it would work. Never had I thought anyone would want to spend time in the Bible with me. But I realized what my Paul was doing was exciting. The sense of peace and faith he had was rubbing off on me.

One of the most impacting things he shared with me, when I was 27 years old, was the concept of "fools' hill." This referred to how young people make the climb up "fools' hill," making foolish decisions and suffering the consequences of those decisions. I later brought it up to him and identified where I saw myself on the climb up the hill. He never told me I had to go up the "hill"; he just told me about it. I now had a picture of where I was. I had been acting like a boy, but now I wanted to become a man. I needed to keep climbing to get up and over "fool's hill" by living my life as I was learning a man should.

Now I have a different view of life. I want to help men around me. I want to be involved with them in my life. I want to have a Christ-centered life and raise my children to have the same. I want to bring people into my home just as my Paul brought me into his.

I hope my story will help older men desire to help younger men in the same way my Paul did for me as my patriarch. Hopefully, I can inspire younger men to seek a patriarch who can help them live a Christ-centered life.

## Scripture references

Ecclesiastes 5:19-20; Ecclesiastes 3:1-14; 1 Corinthians 16:13-14; Isaiah 46:4; Psalm 90:10, 12; Matthew 28:19-20

....................................................................

# Questions for reflection or discussion
....................................................................

What are your comments on this chapter?

What has been your personal experience with this topic?

Any Scriptures or principles discussed in this chapter you need to apply in your life?

# Part III:

*Character Development*

# 24.
# Purpose
....................

*"Our days may come to seventy years, or eighty, if our strength
endures; yet the best of them are but trouble and sorrow, for
they quickly pass, and we fly away. Teach us to number our
days aright, that we may gain a heart of wisdom."*
*Psalm 90:10-12*

### Paul's perspective

The older I get the more it seems that time flies by faster and faster.
One of my dad's favorite sayings, "We are making great time, too bad we
don't know where we are going," expresses the dilemma of many (if not
most) people with regard to a clear purpose for their lives.

Jesus led a purposed life. He is the best model for purpose because
He knew exactly why He had come, and why He was here. He knew what
His work was, He accomplished His purpose here, and then He left. For
us, it should be the same. But most of us don't give much thought to why
we are here or for how long. The Scriptures encourage us to examine
how long we will be here so that we might have a wise perspective. Purpose begins when we start to understand God has put us here and has
things He wants us to accomplish. Until men establish purpose for their
lives, they usually give their lives to the three C's: count, control, and col-
lect. Men struggle because we tend to think we are here to make a lot of
money, set ourselves above others, and conquer things. As long as we are
trying to serve more than one purpose, or one master, we will struggle
with what our purpose really is.

My time with men in the discipleship process has revealed that men
find it extremely difficult to establish a clear purpose for their lives. There
are many fine books and study guides written on this subject, but more

often than not they leave men unable to get committed to a purpose, at least one that is written and clearly defined.

Without purpose, men's lives are chaotic; they lack the single-minded commitment needed to become faithful instruments for performing the work God has for them. The death to self-interest in one's life is a critical common denominator for effective Timothys and future Pauls. With this element in place, God begins to work in a man and use him effectively. As Timothy observes men who are dead to their self-interest and motivated out of a desire to serve God and others, he should begin taking a serious look at his own self-interest, ineffective ministry and purposeless life. He will discover that he has little joy in his labors, and no amount of hard work will produce the fruit only God can give – through a man committed to God's purpose for his life, one that is "dead" to his own selfish motivations.

It's best for me to let Timothy know my life's purpose and leave him to wrestle with his purpose. The simple act of writing the purpose statement down for most men means they are going to be accountable to it. But committing one's life to a specific, clearly thought-out purpose is difficult for men. They are uncertain they want to be accountable to God, because this narrows the playing field and limits their free will to live as they please, to be able to jump into any enticing situation that may present itself.

I am convinced that what holds many men back is a fear deep within – a fear that they don't have what it takes to fulfill God's purpose for their lives. Therefore they hold back on a written commitment to a life purpose.

Major Ian Thomas has written about a disciple in his book, *The Indwelling Life of Christ:* "Death to all that he is in his own inadequacy is the only gateway through which he may enter the fullness of all that Christ is, so he may live miraculously in the power of His resurrection. Death to self and self-interests is the price a man must pay to be raised from the dead works of his flesh that prevent him from committing to a God-given purpose for his life. Until a man has the willingness to die to self, he will never become what he is intended to be. If he is not wholly convinced that Christ is willing and able to take over, unbelief will rear its ugly head and prevent him from allowing Jesus to assume responsibility for his life."

A God-given, inspired purpose for my life begins when I realize that life is not about me – that is, being self-centered, focused on what am I doing for me, and what is going to take place in my life. As long as I am me-centered, rather than God-centered, a fruitful, purposed life is at the furthest extreme of what I would hope to experience.

As I disciple Timothy, he will be observing my life and drawing conclusions about the purpose of my life. I will communicate to him that I have a written purpose statement and hope that he will do the same when he is ready. Currently I have been meeting with a man for several years, and for the past three months he has been promising to work out the purpose for his life. Periodically I check in with him, just to encourage him. He keeps telling me he wants to get back to it, but the fact is, he is still serving his self-interests and is stuck right there.

I encourage Timothy to come into a place where he decides it is more important to serve Christ than what he has been serving. Men must sit down with God, talk it through, and ask what life is going to look like when it is finished. Finally, men must ask God what to labor toward. The things Jesus said are very purposeful and if we address them face-to-face with Him, the result leads to an inspired, purposeful, fulfilling life.

When a purpose statement is written down, it will change Timothy's life. Now he can begin to say no to the plethora of pursuits he could give his life to that do not benefit his purpose. He can choose to do *good* things, choose to do *better* things, or choose to do the *best* things with his time. There are many choices in the Christian smorgasbord of good things that he may be called to, including such options as women's pregnancy centers, helping the poor, prison ministries, mission trips, one–on-one discipleship, etc. All of which are really good works to which he could choose to give his life. However, when he becomes committed with a written purpose statement, many of his issues – especially fear of the future – will begin to disappear. That is because it becomes easy to say no to things outside of his written purpose, making his life simpler, more ordered, and usually less stressful. Knowing why you are here, and what God has uniquely equipped you to do, can free you from the pressures of the multiple demands and opportunities that confront us every day.

## Timothy's story

It had been four years since I invited Jesus to come into my life as my Savior so that my wretched sinful soul could be connected to God. The process of learning to follow Jesus was ongoing. I did not know much about Jesus, since it had been 25 years since I was last around the Bible as a teenager. Now I was fortunate to be sitting before good Bible teachers. My hunger for reading spiritual literature and listening to recordings of quality teaching was helping me to gain a clear picture of what a Christian's life and walk should be like. As I developed relationships through my Paul with several Christ-centered businessmen, it became evident they had clear purpose for their lives. I was cautious about buying into another man's purpose, since I had done that several times in the past and it had proven to be a mistake. I was sure I did not need to be a copycat in adopting a purpose for my life.

My Paul wisely did not attempt to steer me in a direction, but let me wrestle with my decision. For several years I studied books written on the subject while my purposeless thinking jumped from one idea to the next about my life's direction.

In 1987, I experienced the beginning of major business failure and came to the end of my all-out pursuit of secular business success. I planned to continue my career and line of work, real estate brokerage, but would limit my hours and commitment to my profession. I was ready "to seek first His Kingdom." Now God through the Scriptures spoke clearly to me, and I concluded the purpose of my life would be "to know Christ and make Him known." My life would be a spiritual sacrifice to God. I would give up my self-interests for the interest of God. I would no longer copy the ways of worldly men, and asked God to transform me into a new man, able to know His will for my life.

I have lived this purpose for 20-plus years and it has proven to be an incredible steadying force for me. I have been through some life storms that could have distracted me, but having a purpose of knowing Christ and making Him known has kept me afloat and able to live a life that I could make sense of. Without a purpose I would have been like a rudderless ship blown around by life's ever-shifting winds to places and circumstances that made little sense. Because of my purpose, however, I have been able to accept God's providence and have learned that He knows what is good for me better than I do.

## Scripture references

Proverbs 29:18a (KJV); Esther 4:16; 2 Corinthians 13:5; John 17:3,4; Psalms 90:10, 12; Matthew 6:24; John 6:27; Matthew 6:33; Romans 12:1-2

......................................................................
# *Questions for reflection or discussion*
......................................................................

What are your comments on this chapter?

What has been your personal experience with this topic?

Any Scriptures or principles discussed in this chapter you need to apply in your life?

# 25.
# Truth

..............

*"Sanctify them by the truth, your word is truth."*
John 17:17

## Paul's perspective

Discovering the truth can set a man free, and Jesus proclaims in John 14:6 that He is the truth. Truth is not an option, something that evolves over time, nor is it a concept. Truth is Jesus Christ, who comes to live in us and direct us in the ways of God as we become totally dependent upon Him.

As I meet with Timothy and he shares his failures, I am hopeful he will be motivated to change his worldview from one based on his relative truth to one based on God's truth as found in the Bible. Having a Kingdom-based view of the world is necessary if Timothy is to be transformed by the renewing of his mind. This transformation will lead him to an intimate, indwelling relationship with Christ, a new set of values, and a change in his behavior.

My relationship with Timothy exposes me to his truth. He has been subjected to the brainwashing of a culture that often portrays unrighteousness as righteousness. Little by little I get to know his view of truth. I am careful to listen – and slow to speak or debate. His truth is based on a composite of his experiences in life. In his worldview he may have himself and his needs at the center, or he may have God at the center. Having himself at the center of his world produces a relativistic form of the truth. By relativism, I mean that whatever I see as good for me is my truth. When a man bases the decisions for his life on his relative truths, as opposed to God's truth, he continually fails and has to regroup and start over.

The common ground between men is our secular, fallen nature. It is here Timothy and I can relate. If I am someone he sees only as being spiritual all the time, this poses a problem in his ability to connect with me. The only difference between a lost person and me is that Christ has come and taken His place in me. I still have my old, fallen nature. This nature has been trained by a fallen world to follow the world's truths that are usually opposite of God's Kingdom truth. Being transparent with Timothy about my fallen nature and struggles is necessary for us to connect and establish common ground.

Most secular men are unaware, or unwilling to admit, they have a lot of false crutches on which they lean. In the evangelical process, we uncover these crutches that keep him from identifying with Christ. Little by little through our relationships, we can remove those untrue crutches. Because our fallen natures are the same, but my worldview is based on Christ, I can still relate to him and help him to set aside the crutches that keep him from the truth of Christ. This helps him to change his thinking from secular to spiritual. Effective evangelism relates to a man's fallen nature and helps him begin to think through the issues of truth for his life. I don't necessarily give him the answers. It's best that he comes to his own conclusions, convicted by the Scriptures and the power of the Holy Spirit. When he discovers, embraces and applies Kingdom truth, I affirm him and we rejoice in the renewing of his mind.

Timothy has relied on the world system for direction and values concerning politics, business, recreation, religion, social acceptance, female conquest, position, and title. As he experiences failure, he eventually discovers there is no lasting truth he can count on by trusting in the world's system. It no longer makes sense to him as he struggles to recover from failures and chart a new course for himself.

As I am able to get close enough to him that he can see my Kingdom way of living, he is attracted to how I am living and the person who is in me, that being Jesus Christ. Up to this point, he has created his own standards, which are moveable so he can do anything he wants with them. Now, as he realizes there is a greater standard than his own, he begins to grow and change. The Kingdom truth leads him to Kingdom-based worldview, values and behavior. Timothy's Kingdom truth discovery process often begins when he meets with me and will continue throughout his life as he meets with his own Timothys, discovering and rediscovering this truth.

## Timothy's story

At age forty, I was a desperate man and my life was not going the way I had planned. Two major business failures, a divorce, and a failing second marriage had me rethinking the truth I had embraced. I had done what I thought would be good for me, but kept coming up short and having to start over. I determined I needed to find real truth, which I believed had to exist somewhere in the universe. To that end I read a lot of self-help books and examined a few religions and philosophies.

The light came on when I discovered Jesus in the first four books of the New Testament. I liked Him right away. He was bold, honest, and a really good man. His truth made sense to me. I became convicted about my fallen nature. I was a cheater, liar, and downright dishonest in the way I conducted many of the affairs of my life. At this point I confessed my sins, invited Jesus into my life as my Savior, and was what the Bible calls "born again." I began to become a student of the Bible, attending church-type activities. A couple of years after my conversion, I met my Paul and we began meeting. I started watching and listening to him, at the same time examining my own ways of approaching life as opposed to his ways. I was beginning to see my ways were still based on my secular worldview values that I had brought with me into the Kingdom. Regrettably, I fought hard to hold onto many of these old values and the accompanying behavior. I often wanted my Paul to debate with me, but he seldom entered into debate over our different behaviors and perspectives.

I continued to hold onto my hard-charging, manipulating, worldly success-motivated personality. So God used brokenness – hardships in my life to convict me of my need to understand that His truth was the only real truth. I experienced brokenness in my marriage as we struggled to live together. The truth was that I was an ungodly, worldly behaving husband who needed to change before my wife could be changed by God. I observed my Paul's marriage and learned from what I saw; slowly I began to change, resulting in my wife's own changes. Now we have a solid, Christ-centered marriage.

Another area where I experienced brokenness was in our finances. For years I spent more than I made and borrowed to make up the difference.

We experienced hard times and lived from commission check to commission check, often having no money to pay the overdue bills. As I studied what God has to say in the Scriptures about money, observed how my Paul and his wife handled money, and saw the vast differences between our financial circumstances, it was clear he was following God's truth and I was not. It has taken years for us to work our way out of financial chaos, but we have become better stewards of God's money. Today we are debt-free with reserves in the bank, no longer being servants to the lenders.

I also experienced brokenness in my business, in raising children and in ministry, to name just a few. In every case, the untrue secular worldview I held as I came into a saving relationship with Christ had to be transformed by God's truth. I could read about it in the Scriptures, but the changes came most often when I saw God's truth being lived out, up close and personal, in my Paul's life.

### Scripture references
Ecclesiastes 3:7b: John 17:17: Romans 12:2; John 14:6

...............................................................................

## Questions for reflection or discussion
...............................................................................

What are your comments on this chapter?


What has been your personal experience with this topic?


Any Scriptures or principles discussed in this chapter you need to apply in your life?

# 26.
# Focus
. . . . . . . . . . . . . . .

*"I have fought the good fight, I have finished
the race, I have kept the faith."*
*2 Timothy 4:7*

## Paul's perspective

Once the discipleship one-on-one process begins, the Timothy might remain on earth another 30-40 years, perhaps longer. However long it is, the apostle Paul warns these years will be a struggle. During that span a man continues to battle with his own flesh and the forces of evil. How a man starts the process is not as important as how he finishes. Over this long period of time he becomes a Paul and many changes will take place in his life. If he is to stay purpose-directed, concentrating on his goal of making disciples rather than making money, he will need to be focused.

Focus is essential to the process of becoming a spiritually mature man. Men I have discipled are usually struggling with focus in two ways: They are either focused on one thing at the expense of everything else, or they are unfocused and tossed about by the random, unpredictable events of their day. Balance is a goal of the life available for God's use in his Kingdom work. When a man comes into Christ he is usually scattered, trying to do 10-15 things at once, not focused, and concerned about how he is going to provide for himself. He has yet to realize that God is the one who provides. The new believer's perspective may be that only professional clergy can be disciplemakers, when the truth is that a businessman often does the work of one-on-one discipling more effectively than a pastor.

As a Paul, I am responsible to help Timothy begin to focus, first by modeling focus in my life, and encouraging him to concentrate on a few things, especially those that have eternal value, such as men's souls and

God's truth. My job is to help him, little by little, set aside foolish things and move from being a boy to becoming a man focused on living in truth.

The struggle with focus begins initially when we start meeting and scheduling our time together. I have made a commitment to be available to the man when he is available. For a few men this is a big challenge because they are not living a scheduled life. For others, however, finding a suitable time is simple since they are accustomed to scheduling their lives and have the freedom to do so. Then there are men living a life where someone else is scheduling their lives for them.

Often men are working more than 10 hours a day. Finding time to meet is a challenge for them, so we might have to meet on the weekend. Over a period of time, men learn to schedule time with me and make it a priority. Either that or the process stagnates.

I observe men's behavior according to what I like to call the "FAT Man" criteria, as mentioned earlier. This has nothing to do with his weight; it is about his character and its development. The "FAT Man" is one who is (F) *faithful,* which means he does what he commits to do. He is also (A) *available,* this means he is able to prioritize our time together and not be so committed to other things that our time gets passed over. Thirdly, he is (T) *teachable.* A teachable man is capable of grasping Biblical truth that will modify his old worldly truths. This man is one who is willing to take the action necessary and to apply Biblical truth to his life by modifying his behavior. So by our definition, a "FAT Man" is one who is *faithful, available,* and *teachable.*

The initial phase of the discipleship process begins with the building of a comfortable relationship between Timothy and me. At some point we get into the Bible and I use a set of books known as *Operation Timothy* (available from www.cbmc.com). These books examine the foundational aspects of the life of a follower of Christ. We usually spend two or more years in these books during our weekly or biweekly meetings, as his schedule allows. In the latter stage of this process of working through the books together, we begin to pray for a man for Timothy to meet with and disciple.

When Timothy finds a man to meet with (this might happen right away or it may take him several years to find someone), he begins the process I have modeled for him with that new man. Sadly, some men never find anyone, and after a few years the spiritual maturity they have obtained begins to wane and, as a result, spiritual atrophy often sets in. If you are to finish the race, you have to use what you have learned – or you lose it. Like strengthening a muscle, if you don't continue to exercise it you will see the strength you gained start to decline.

Therefore in my heart I have established as a priority the commitment to stay in the search with Timothy, helping him in finding a man to meet with. Without a man to disciple, he is not going to grow properly. It is spiritually unhealthy to keep what you have learned and not give it away. In the New International Version of the Bible, Philemon 6 says, "I pray that you may be active in sharing your faith, so that you will have a full understanding of every good thing we have in Christ." In other words, "sharing our faith" through a disciplemaking relationship is part of God's process for enabling us to understand His truth more fully.

When I first started meeting with men, I thought I was engaged in the process for *their* benefit. Five or six years into the process I realized God had me doing this because He wanted to grow *me* up in my relationship with Christ. This would not happen unless I was imparting my life – and the life of Christ in me – to another person. I have heard it said you only have what you give away, so if you keep it to yourself you will lose it.

Once Timothy becomes a Paul, inevitably he will come under attack from the enemy. He still has me for support, but he needs to get involved with a small group of men who all are Pauls and undergoing similar experiences with their own Timothys.

The Jesus, Paul, Timothy (JPT) relationship is often a lifelong relationship. The relationships with other Pauls hopefully also will continue in the life of a Paul as he strives to maintain his focus, that of making disciples.

## Timothy's story

Like many men, I spent most of the first 30 years of my life in an unfocused way. My vision was limited to what I would eat at the next meal, which girl might be interested in me, and which sport I would play the next season. I also tried to achieve success in school, so I set goals each semester to try and make A's and B's. And in my striving to be a "good guy," I always went to church and tried to hang out with other good people. My overall life goal was simple: to be a good athlete, a good student, and just an all-around nice guy that everyone liked. Looking back, I see now that I was just really driven by the need to hear my father say, "Well done." Moving into college and graduate school, the vision changed slightly and I became more focused on my career. But I had no long-term plan and purpose, so life became a series of reactions to one crisis after another.

Getting married and having our first child, while working at establishing myself as a young lawyer, all began to take a toll. We had no long-term plans as a family, as I frankly did not know how to be a husband, father, and leader of my family. We had no budget and spent everything we earned. Life became a daily grind of get up, go to work, come home, eat dinner, help with the baby, get a few hours of sleep, and back at it again the next day.

In the summer of 1991, when my son was just a few months old, I was introduced to an older guy who had been looking for someone to disciple for a couple of years. Up to this point my life wasn't exactly a model of consistency. I had gone to three colleges in four years, two law schools in three years, and was about to change jobs for the second time in two years. When I met my first "Paul" at age 27, I found out for the first time in my life what a true friend looked like. This guy spent time with me and modeled unconditional love, grace and acceptance. I questioned how he could do that. I knew about "God" and that "Jesus was His Son," but as this guy lived his life in front of me authentically, sharing struggles and successes, and as he introduced me to other guys like him, I began to see that their lives had a focus that mine did not.

After a year of meeting with this first Paul, the Scriptures we learned and the love and acceptance I felt from him had dissolved my hard religious exterior to where I knew I needed a relationship with Christ. I was tired of being a religious fake. In September 2002, I prayed to receive Christ. I continued meeting with my first Paul, and he continued modeling the same focus on Christ, investing time in me and a few other guys, as well as his family. I also saw how he worked at ordering his life, how he spent his time and money, but yet maintained his primary focus on experiencing and modeling intimacy with Christ.

After a few years, I was introduced to another guy who was also a "Paul." He led a small group that I joined where he challenged me – at times in a bold and honest way I had not seen before – and yet always with an attitude of caring for me. I continued meeting with my first Paul, but this other guy became a close friend, too. He urged me to work on healing my relationship with my father. He also took us into a study of the Bible in such depth that I had never seen before.

As he did all this, he transparently shared his struggles with his marriage, his own father, and his work. God was not in a box with this guy. This was a daily, living and focused relationship. One of his sayings, I will never forget, was "Seek God and men's souls" and let God take care of your needs. He really lived out, in front of me, the truth of Matthew 6:33.

I later left that group and joined another that was led by a lawyer like me, who also had been struggling with his marriage and career. He encouraged me to "get in the pit and suffer" with my wife, and that the Christ who lived in me would give me the strength. I also watched him live this out in front of me.

A few years after that, I met with several guys who had a great impact on me. These guys ranged from a few years older than me to 20 years older than I was, but the common thread with them was the pursuit of intimacy with Christ, along with the pursuit of men to disciple. This was a focused lifestyle with these guys.

By this time I had grown tired of disorder in my career and finances, and had made progress in my marriage, but still had a way to go in becoming a true leader at home. These guys heard that from me and never let up, challenging and exhorting me to take concrete steps to get order in these areas. I could see that without an intentional pursuit of order in my life, I would continue to struggle with maintaining focus on my walk with Christ and my availability to people, including men God brought along my path to invest in.

There are a number of other mature men I have met through the relationships I described earlier, and these men also have rubbed off on me in positive ways. I have seen their focus on Jesus and winning and discipling guys, all the while loving their wives and families and taking care of their finances and careers in an ordered and diligent way.

God is continuing to change my heart as a result of these relationships, so that now my desire also is to grow deeper with Christ and to pursue men's souls. Work is now more of a support tool than the primary focus it was when I started 20 years ago. God has used all of these men to help me focus on eternal things. I will always be grateful that these guys made themselves available to God to be used by Him to bring focus into my life.

### Scripture references
2 Timothy 4:7; Hebrews 13:5; James 1:5-6; Philippians 3:12-14; 1 John 1:5-7; Proverbs 27:17; Matthew 6:33: Hebrews 10:24-25

........................................................................

## *Questions for reflection or discussion*
........................................................................

What are your comments on this chapter?

What has been your personal experience with this topic?

Any Scriptures or principles discussed in this chapter you need to apply in your life?

# 27.
# Fear
.............

*"So do not fear, for I am with you; do not be dismayed, for
I am your God. I will strengthen you and help you; I
will uphold you with my righteous right hand."*
Isaiah 41:10

## Paul's perspective

God encourages us not to fear or be dismayed because He will hold us up through our relationship with Jesus. He promises to provide and meet all of our needs. He did not spare His own Son but gave Him up for all of us and will graciously give us all things we need. It is by faith in Jesus that our fears, burdens and weariness can be replaced with the rest and peace for our souls that He promises.

One of my greatest fears was the fear of death. As a little kid I heard others say death meant a box in the ground where my body would become covered by worms eating my rotting flesh. This hopeless thought haunted me until age 40 when, through reading Scriptures, I came to the understanding that God gives me eternal life in His Son. Once I had faith that I had Him as my Savior, I was set free from the fear of death.

Fear isn't always a bad thing. It is mentioned in Proverbs that the fear of the Lord is the beginning of wisdom. Fear can be an emotional feeling or it can be intellectual. Helping Timothy deal with his fears is a natural part of the one-on-one discipleship process. As I share with him my fears, he can feel safe in sharing his. We can examine our fears in light of Biblical truth and pray for God to bring us emotional peace and intellectual understanding. Moving from fear to faith is a process we will experience over and over throughout our lives.

Experience has taught me that the world is moving along a path and toward a destination way beyond my control or even my understanding.

This macro-perspective is something I can pray about, yet not something I have any discernible impact upon. Because I am unable to control these matters, they are a possible source of fear. Timothy and I can choose, however, to focus on the micro-perspective – those things upon which we can make an impact. This does not mean that I am not interested in the macro (big scale) events of the world. It does mean we should devote most of our time, energy and thoughts to those micro-events falling within our sphere of influence. All concerns are an opportunity for Timothy and me to trust in God and be amazed as He reveals His perfect plan to us over time.

As Timothy and I focus on the few things we do have some influence over, we discover we're at the mercy of God to oversee all things and meet our needs as we labor to manage our own daily decisions and affairs. Even taking a risk can be a fearful thing. The courage necessary for risk-taking comes with true faith and a deeply seated belief that, regardless of the outcome, God is walking with us every step of the way.

As Timothy and I walk through life together, a God-focused relationship begins to develop, through which we find God guiding and taking care of us. The fears of today are replaced by being able to rejoice in God's control and provisions, regardless of the circumstances. We come to know that opportunities for trusting God await us just around the corner or down the road. And it never ends – the process of moving from fear to faith will be with us until we leave this life for a better one.

Fear comes in a number of different forms and degrees. Concern might be one description of lesser fear. Other forms might be described as being anxious, vexed, worried, distressed, perturbed, upset, or disturbed. More major, more emotionally charged fear quickly transforms into dread, terror, panic, alarm, dismay, or just plain feeling scared. Whatever the degree, fear is not a pleasant experience.

The things men fear are endless and unique to each individual. A few examples of common fears would be: losing, taking risks, lack of understanding, judgment, running out of money, lack of achievement, the unknown, and poor performance. Once Timothy becomes open to expressing and confessing his fears, God can begin the process of replacing the apprehension and negative feelings into a positive – an enduring, unconditional trust in Him.

Prolonged fear makes men sick, both mentally and physically. Treatment of fear by medication or other forms of therapy is a major business in United States, yet Scriptures indicate God intends fear to be a warning that we have veered off the path of trusting Him. He installed fear in man's makeup, much like an automobile manufacturer installs a red light on the dashboard as a warning that something needs our attention. Fear is a good thing if we pay attention to it as a signal and take appropriate action. That action is a return to living by faith in God's goodness and sovereignty.

The best way I can help Timothy overcome fear is by being transparent with Him about my own struggles with fear, and the process I needed for learning to trust in the Lord and leaning not on my own understanding. Living by faith and living according to the Word of God in front of Timothy will be of great value for both him and me.

## Timothy's story

I grew up in a home dominated by an undercurrent of fear. Fear was the primary motivator for most decisions my parents made, and therefore it became deeply ingrained in my worldly decision-making process. Living in fear, I learned, is a painfully debilitating existence.

Several years ago I was going through a custody battle with the mother of my two children, a son and newborn daughter. The courts in my hometown had given me custody of both children. My son was living with me, but my daughter was out of state and I had no idea where.

The court battle was a long, drawn-out, stress-filled process that left me exhausted. When it finally ended, I was relieved the legal proceedings were over, but the fear and anxiety experienced throughout the process and not knowing if I would get custody was overwhelming, with lasting consequences.

As I met with my Paul, we prayed to God and asked Him to do what He thought was best for my children. Knowing that the children ultimately are His helped relieve some of the fear I carried from one moment to the next, yet the struggle was there on an ongoing basis. As I learned more about Christ and His desires for me through the Paul-Timothy relationship, I began to fully realize who I was as a Christian and how I had been changed when I asked Christ into my life. As I grew in a relationship with Christ, I began to understand that surrendering my life to Christ could provide the desired relief from my fearful human nature.

In December 2003, I had a practical opportunity to apply this understanding. Without any idea of where my daughter was located, I received the final court order allowing me to go and get her. I had a couple of addresses where she might be, so I quickly packed and got ready to leave town and begin my search. But then my attorney received a phone call from their mother from an unfamiliar number. From this new phone number we were able to identify a new address as a possible location for my daughter.

So I headed out with the court order, this new address in hand. I was hoping we would find her and be able to bring her back to my state. First, we had to convince the authorities in this other state that we had a right to this child. I arrived in a small town and quickly took our case into the court system. A hearing was required to show I had the custodial right to take my daughter back to our home state. During the entire time we were fearful, but hopeful, that the mother would not discover we were there and attempt to move my daughter to a new location.

The process with the local legal system was complicated and time-consuming. There were delays and various processes to work through. Once my document was recognized as valid, the state required it be re-recorded before authorities would assist me in assuming possession. During these delays at the courthouse, we bumped into my daughter's mother. She took one look at us and sped on down the street in her car. I remember praying, feeling that was it. That I was not going to see my daughter again.

I feared I was going to be tied up with the necessary legal proceedings while the mother's illegal choices would prevail, ultimately resulting in the loss of my child. Filled with a tremendous amount of fear, I sat in the courthouse on the third floor, praying and silently crying out to God. When I opened my eyes and lifted my head, there was a bright red ladybug crawling across the floor. I had always associated ladybugs with good luck, so I thought that was a sign from God that everything was going to be okay because He was in control. Shortly afterward the court secretary appeared with the document; the recording of the paperwork was finalized.

I went down to the sheriff's office with the document. He asked where I wanted to go. I gave him the address of the new location discovered through the mother's phone. We drove up into the mountains to a remote area and found the address. The sheriff walked up to the house and came out with my daughter. I remember being amazed at the peace I received through prayer, trusting Christ, and the appearance of a God-sent ladybug.

## Scripture references

Isaiah 41:10; Joshua 1:9; Proverbs 1:7; Philippians 4:19; 1 John 5:11-13; Proverbs 3:5-6; Romans 8:32; Matthew 11:28-30

. . . . . . . . . . . . . . . . . . . . . . . . . . . . . . . . . . . . . . . . . . . . . . . . . . . . . . . . . . . . .

## Questions for reflection or discussion

. . . . . . . . . . . . . . . . . . . . . . . . . . . . . . . . . . . . . . . . . . . . . . . . . . . . . . . . . . . . .

What are your comments on this chapter?

What has been your personal experience with this topic?

Any Scriptures or principles discussed in this chapter you need to apply in your life?

# 28.
# Anger
.................

*"My dear brothers, take note of this: Everyone should be quick
to listen, slow to speak and slow to become angry, for man's
anger does not bring about the righteous life that God desires."*
James 1:19-20

## *Paul's perspective*

The basic truth about anger is that we all experience it. So a significant part of the discipleship process in meeting with Timothy is dealing
with his anger. The root cause of anger stems from past hurts. Things
from his past that have hurt him, as well as things presently going on
in his life, can be addressed and healed as his transparency allows these
hurts to surface.

Anger can be passive and under the surface, thus not easily detected.
His active anger will be easy to see, however, enabling us to address those
issues and pray for healing. Often some of Timothy's anger has become
resentment. At the bottom of his emotional cup are resentments that
have deepened into bitterness. This bitterness usually is deep-rooted,
and it may take a long time before he will experience freedom and healing.

Forgiveness is the road Timothy must travel if he is to be successful in learning to address and overcome anger, resentment and bitterness. Typically the cause of our anger involves people. In many cases,
anger originates in unresolved conflict involving the family of origin.
Because such negative feelings are long-standing, they turn into bitterness. Timothy must be willing to forgive people if he is to be freed from
these unhealthy attitudes.

Few people recognize that they are angry with God. After all, He is
sovereign over all things and He has allowed whatever it is that is causing

the anger. A healthy start in dealing with anger begins with thanking God for the anger-causing situation, with the knowledge He has allowed – or is allowing – the situation for reasons beyond our understanding. Trusting God is where we start. Forgiving people becomes easier as Timothy grows in his recognition of the depth of his own depravity. I can help this process along by being transparent about my own depravity. Christ has died for the forgiveness of our sin and the sins of others. As He forgave us, we must also forgive others and ourselves.

Media coverage of today's culture seems to be a source of anger for many. Political, moral, religious, financial and other issues are often reported in such a manner that they generate anger within readers and viewers. Many are addicted to non-stop news reports, yet feel angered by the reporters' non-objective spin. Timothy and I must live where "the prince of this world" rules and if we buy into worldly perspectives, we can feel burdened and angered. I must model for Timothy a trust in God to demonstrate His sovereignty over the things of the world and keep my focus on the priceless, eternal things of knowing Christ and making Him known.

Anger, whether intellectual or emotional, affects our physical and mental well-being. Anger turned inward is the definition of depression. We live in a culture filled with depressed people whose anger has gone deep down, sometimes beyond reach. These people are often at a loss when it comes to dealing with this type of anger. Because of this, prescription drugs have become a big business in our culture because they seem to relieve (or at least conceal) this deep-down anger. People also self-medicate by abusing substances like alcohol, illegal drugs, and food. Other forms of abuse – pornography, gambling, excessive spending, TV watching, and addiction to work or exercise – are other ways of "medicating" anger. Helping Timothy become transparent about his own addictions often leads to healing and freedom from these bondages of his flesh.

One major source of anger for a lot of men is their family members. It often begins with anger toward their father and mother. Anger toward one's earthly father in particular affects their relationship with God, their heavenly Father. The anger-healing process must include dealing with these relationships if healthy, complete healing is to take place. Forgiveness is the key element for restoring relationships and being delivered from anger being directed toward these key family members.

Often Timothy's anger will be focused on his wife. After a few years of butting heads over different views with regard to finances and child-rearing, just to name two of many common sources of conflict, partners become angry with each other. This anger shows up in many ways during their everyday encounters, wrecking the relationship. In such instances I pray that Timothy can learn to manage his anger by being quick to listen, slow to speak and slow to anger. The modeling of extending to my wife grace and forgiveness is a major challenge for me in the JPT process. My transparency with my own marital struggles will encourage Timothy to stay the course in his marriage with grace and forgiveness.

Every man lives his life either in a state of anger/resentment or forgiveness. Forgiveness is a decision a man must make. If he can become an unconditional forgiver of others, and an acceptor of the circumstances God allows in his life, he can consistently set aside his anger and enjoy the rest and peace God wants him to have.

## Timothy's story

I grew up being pretty comfortable with anger. Dad was often angry with certain people, especially the politicians running the country. They were among his favorites to be angry with. In sports I used my anger to push myself to defeat my opponents. For the most part, I controlled my anger and thought I did a good job of using it to my advantage. My motto could have been, "get angry and succeed."

No doubt a lot of people were impacted by my angry words in both personal and business matters. Often my marriage partner accused me of being a mean person. By the time I reached my mid-30s, I had a lot of acquaintances but few, if any, real friends because of my anger. No one was really willing to get close to me and my constant companion – anger. About this time many things began unraveling, taking my life in a negative direction. My marriage ended. I had a couple of business failures. I was medicating my anger with a combination of unhealthy illegal and legal substances, and destructive lifestyle decisions. I began to experience health issues related to the abuse of my body. This was even more depressing for me, and the idea of suicide entered my mind.

My plan for life was not working, so I began looking for a new way of living. It was during this time I invited Christ to come into my life and take over. I began dealing with and addressing my sinful, dishonest life. I felt racked with envy, jealousy, strife, and the guilt of living like a pagan. I began meeting with my Paul, getting discipled, and gradually began recognizing my sins and confessing them, which in turn resulted in me being delivered from the pain they caused my soul.

I continued to be an angry man, however, holding onto the idea that my anger helped me succeed in the worldly affairs of my life. The government got involved in my business. In the 1980s, new laws were passed initiating the decline and eventual dismantling of the real estate and banking aspects of my business. My investments were rendered worthless, and my ability to make a living also declined.

The government started legal proceedings against me. Their reasoning seemed bogus to me. I became extremely angry, to an extent beyond anything I had ever experienced. This legal process went on for six years. The anger burdened me daily, even entering my dreams. In the middle of the night, I would wake up and wrestle with my angry thoughts for hours. I grew to hate my anger and asked God to deliver me from its burden.

In the end result, I lost my legal battle and was faced with severe penalties. Despite that, at this point God delivered me from my anger. I realized He had allowed these circumstances to occur in my life for reasons I could not understand at the time. Accepting the Lord's sovereignty over the circumstances and events of my life freed me from my anger toward God, myself and the government. This occurred more than 15 years ago and I have lived a life free from the kind of anger that so easily turns into resentment and eventually, bitterness. I still find myself feeling angered for short periods of time, but then quickly remember God is still sovereign and He knows best. This delivers me quickly from anger and allows me to get on with my life, looking to God and trusting Him to take care of me.

## Scripture References

James 1:19-20; Romans 8:1; Ephesians 5:20; Matthew 6:14-15; 1 Corinthians 2:2; James 1:19-20; Isaiah 26:3; 1 Chronicles 29:11-12; Proverbs 3:5-6

## *Questions for reflection or discussion*

What are your comments on this chapter?

What has been your personal experience with this topic?

Any Scriptures or principles discussed in this chapter you need to apply in your life?

# 29.
# Bondage

........................

*"For though we live in the world, we do not wage war as the world does. The weapons we fight with are not the weapons of the world. On the contrary, they have divine power to demolish strongholds. We demolish arguments and every pretension that sets itself up against the knowledge of God, and we take captive every thought to make it obedient to Christ."*
*2 Corinthians 10:3-5*

### Paul's perspective:

We are all engaged in a war between our flesh and the Spirit. Bondages of the flesh are rooted in us over years and years and become addictions. The truths of the Scriptures also wage war against our sin-dominated flesh. The Scriptures are what change us as we become able to follow God's Word and not yield to our sinful flesh. God and His Word provide the power that brings about the change in us.

I had a sexual addiction, lusting in my mind after any woman that caught my eye or with whom I had been with in the past. It was about seven years after becoming a follower of Christ that God finally relieved me of this addiction in a supernatural way. Having lived a life without God for so long, the thing that gave me the most comfort was sex – and it seemed the most important thing I had. The bondage did not leave me quickly, although I did not have any sexual relationships outside my marriage. The old "tapes" – images and thinking I knew I had to dispose of – played on. These destructive memories lingered for a long time and left me with overwhelming feelings of defeat. After what seemed like a long time of praying over this, God relieved me of this bondage.

I have discovered through personal experience that over the years the "natural flesh" of man often acquires numerous forms of bondage that may develop into addictions constantly fed and reinforced by the world and its system. By bondage I am referring to things such as anger, fear, alcohol, nicotine, drugs, gambling, and pornography, to name some of the more obvious destructive ones. But we should also include a few of the less obvious: excessive use of things we regard as positive, such as exercise, work, leisure, food, hobbies, video games, medications, religion, and ministry. The list is much longer. In general, abuse of most anything or any activity, good or bad, can become an addiction and thus becomes bondage of the flesh. Even negative, fearful experiences from the past can enslave us, leading us into a form of bondage to those thoughts.

When any of the actions mentioned above becomes more important than God, it can become an addiction. A man is not able to seek the Kingdom of God first, as we're instructed, because he is so wrapped up in his addictions, seeking them first instead. He goes to them for comfort, to escape from life. His real need is to turn that addiction, that controlling substance or action, over to Christ. Becoming addicted to Christ is not a bad thing when it occurs in a healthy, supernatural way – learning to experience and abide in the indwelling life of Jesus. Seeking to do so in a legalistic manner, however, creates another form of bondage of the flesh.

Change begins to take place only when bondage – the reality of physical, mental or emotional enslavement – is identified. To bring about change, I start by being with Timothy, encouraging him, praying with him and waiting for God to do something that brings him out of his deeply rooted flesh pattern.

Twelve-step programs are one familiar method used our in culture to treat addictions. Successful treatment puts the addicted person into remission or sobriety. However, the bondage remains a part of the person's physical and psychological makeup. The addictive behavior can re-emerge at any time.

I encourage addicted Timothys to familiarize themselves with the twelve-step programs that address codependent behaviors and attend some meetings. Increasing their understanding of codependency will enlighten them to their need for healing. The Word, under the power of the Holy Spirit, has the power to transform men by the renewing of their minds and results in deliverance. Men's minds have been perverted by the world's ways. Men find that the power of the Holy Spirit empowers them to deny the powerful urge to conform to the patterns of the world. Ultimately, they experience supernatural deliverance from their various forms of bondage. As this occurs, they become able to test and approve of God's will, His good, pleasing and perfect will for their lives. The freedom a man experiences from this transformation of his mind usually is reflected by an outward, visible, observable deliverance I have seen over and over in men's lives. One outcome of this freedom is becoming useable to God.

In this war between the flesh and the Spirit, my role with Timothy is to help him become transparent about his bondages and pray for him as he is exposed to the Word and its healing power. Memorizing Scriptures relevant to specific addictions often proves helpful in the process. What a blessing it is for me as I see the change and healing from the front row seat of my relationship with Timothy.

## Timothy's story:

As we move into intimacy with men, a lot of buried, hidden things are revealed once they begin to truly trust their Paul. These things can be brought up out of the deep well of defeat and despair, and in time healing takes place.

I will never forget a particular meeting with my Timothy. It was so difficult for him to share what was going on in his life. He asked me, "You mind if I tell you something that has really troubled me all of my life?" I answered, "Whatever you say is fine with me, and it is between you and me." He then confided, "What I want to tell you happened when I was five years old, while traveling with my parents. I had to use the bathroom and told my father. He stopped at a highway rest stop and I went, by myself, into the men's restroom. I took my pants down and there was a big man, and he sexually abused me in about a minute and a half. This is the most shameful, embarrassing thing – and I have been carrying it with me all my life."

He stood up with tears in his eyes. All I could do was just comfort him there in the restaurant. But this became his breakthrough for dealing with a major life issue. Our relationship had been going on for three or four years, and he finally wanted to get everything out, to become totally clean by sharing this shameful incident, and closing by praying for God's grace and healing power.

This incident had not been a fault of his own; it was not something that he did or could control. It was something so shameful that it had impacted many areas of his life. But once this scarring act against him was brought into the open, the healing that took place in him as he went forward was unbelievable.

The things that happen to men in their early years often turn into some form of bondage. With the safety of a Paul-Timothy relationship, they can move out of their dark places so that healing then has an opportunity to take place. It is only through allowing these painful experiences to be brought into the light of Jesus Christ, dispelling the darkness, that the healing can and does take place.

### Scripture references

2 Corinthians 10:3-5; Ezekiel 11:19-20; Galatians 5:17; Matthew 6:33; Romans 12:1-2; 1 John 1:9

..................................................................................

## Questions for reflection or discussion
..................................................................................

What are your comments on this chapter?


What has been your personal experience with this topic?


Any Scriptures or principles discussed in this chapter you need to apply in your life?

# Part IV:

## *Aspects of the Disciple's Life*

# 30.
# Wife
············

*"Husbands, love your wives, just as Christ loved*
*the church and gave himself up for her."*
*Ephesians 5:25*

## Paul's perspective

The wife plays a major role in the life of the married Timothy. In addition, those who are single or divorced often can be preoccupied with ex-wives or their quest to find a wife. For that reason, addressing wife-related issues is usually a major aspect of the discipleship process.

We see a marked difference in our movement in the discipling of men: single, divorced, married, and married with children. God has put women in men's lives for very specific reasons, one being to take part in the process of maturing him in Christ. She is there watching him and aware of what he does, with a discerning eye. This can have a positive effect, or she can become an irritating spur in his side. Because the thought processes for women and men is often very different, struggles arise concerning what makes sense in the marriage. Single men without children, by comparison, have no critical eyes through which to see themselves. They go home at night and serve as their own critics. The Paul can take the role of helping them look at their life, but without the presence of a wife, the process can be very different.

Sad but true, a man's relationship with his wife can be a source of suffering for both of them, especially when one of them starts to grow in matters of faith. There are usually many differences in their view of spiritual maturity, and this creates tension and disagreements. The enemy brings about this suffering as he attacks the woman in a marriage, courtship, or divorce situation. The good news is that the man can begin to grow in character and the fruit of the Holy Spirit in response to this adversity. God does not waste suffering in building a disciple. He uses it to tear down old, ungodly ways, replacing them with the character of Christ.

At some point it is important that my wife and I meet with Timothy and his wife, preferably at a restaurant – a neutral site that keeps the wives from having to host a meal and allows both of them to relax. The next step is to have them into our home for a meal at an appropriate later date.

Initially, many wives are suspicious of me as they may not understand the nature of the new relationship their husband, my Timothy, is developing. To her I am stranger changing her husband, their life, and routine. More than likely, the wife is wondering what intimate details of their lives the husband may be sharing with this guy. Along with that, she sees him adding new commitments to his life: Bible study, meeting with men, more "religious" activities. She's aware he needed fixing in certain ways, but wonders whether he has gone off the deep end with this holy stuff. Whether she is religious or not, she may feel threatened, worried that he is replacing her as his first love with Jesus – or this man. It will take some time before his wife begins to see the value of a new Christ-centered husband. To help this along, and minimize potential conflict, he can cut back on some of his other commitments, activities of lesser value that compete for his time with her.

Because wives are typically responders, the change in her attitude toward his spiritual growth becomes more positive as she sees and experiences her husband loving her sacrificially as a byproduct of the discipleship process with his Paul. I have experienced a situation where a husband that had been unfaithful to his wife came to know Christ, repented, and the faithful wife chose to stay with him. As I began to meet with him, the wife became very jealous of our relationship, almost as if I were competing with her. It took more than a year for her to see the love of Christ being more fully formed in him and growing as he continued meeting with me. She knew I was trying to help him, but emotionally it was very difficult for her, especially during the initial months of his discipleship relationship.

Experience has shown me that in most marriages the partners have learned to manipulate each other to get their needs met. My role with Timothy is to help him identify his own manipulations. Men like to use logic to control their wives, and as they grow in Christ they must begin to die to that way of living with her. Since women often try to manipulate and control with their emotions, resulting in arguments and conflict, learning to deal with her feelings is an area Timothy and I spend time talking and praying about. These fights may last for days, weeks or even longer, and because he is not able to handle her emotional outbursts he responds by getting emotional with her. Helping him learn to deal with his wife's emotions and reconcile with her quickly is another critical aspect of Timothy's discipleship.

A major battle that emerges with men and their wives in our female-empowered culture is the husband's role as the spiritual overseer of his family. Many times the guy is out in the work world, consumed with making a living, while the wife is at home, full-time or part-time, taking care of the money and family. If the man has not functioned as the overseer of his family, the wife may well have stepped up and assumed that role in their marriage. Some wives may gladly turn over this leadership role; for others it may take years of battling over who is going to lead the family. She may feel that he has not earned the right to lead, based on past experiences and failures. The changing of her heart and mind is a work God must accomplish; no amount of effort on Timothy's part, trying to change her, will be effective over the long run. When she decides to allow him to assume his rightful role, a great change will occur in the husband-wife relationship and bring glory to God in a wonderful way.

In many cases, men's role models for leading a wife have been absent or dysfunctional. In my own case, it was important to observe my Paul leading his wife. As I was around them for many years, I learned from him how to properly lead my wife. Until then I really had no clue. I would act like a student, go over to his house to see what he did and said, talk with him about it, and little by little I learned from him. He also encouraged me to read books on marriage, and when I took one home and put it on my nightstand, this communicated to my wife I was interested in how to understand and work with her.

I had a heart to learn, watching my Paul and his wife, seeing how they dealt with disagreements and conflict, finances, children, and how a Christ-centered marriage should work. I have observed people in a lot of religious marriages that spent time attending events. However, they would spend little if any time in the homes of positive role models that could teach them in real-life, practical ways to live with each other.

It is very difficult to grow as a wife or husband and understand how to make a marriage work if you have no role models. I believe this lack of healthy husband-wife examples is at the core of the 60-percent divorce rate among first marriages, both for Christians and non-Christians. Helping Timothy accept and learn from his Paul's role model in marriage is another critical event in his discipleship.

In a marriage, each partner has certain areas that, in accordance to their abilities, they may take the lead. These include nurturing the children, home maintenance, record-keeping, and everything else that is necessary to keep a marriage, family and home functioning properly. The spiritual leadership role is assigned by the Lord to the man, however, and he should determine how and where the family can best follow God. As the spiritual leader, he is to be proactive and on his knees, seeking God's will for the family's spiritual maturity. Timothy should expect God will speak to him and be faithful to direct him as he oversees the wife and family.

As a man spiritually matures and becomes more proactive with his faith, he may experience resistance from his wife, especially if she interprets his good work for God as a newfound lover, becoming more important to him than she is. After all, his new activities are taking time, energy and resources. She may limit him by her degree of willingness to support what he is doing. Her willingness to go along with him – or insistence on putting up roadblocks – will determine how far a man can advance with his ministry to other men.

When both enter into the discipleship process, a new perspective of the husband-wife relationship can develop. They can begin to see each other as brother and sister in Christ first and foremost, co-laboring as best friends for the cause of the Gospel.

### Timothy's story

My Paul and I had been meeting for several years before I met my wife, so there was very little resentment toward him. It was, however, pointed out to me by my Paul that my wife would define my ministry. This concept was a struggle for me to comprehend, as I thought it would be God who would define it. What I have come to realize, after 13 years of marriage, is how well a husband ministers to his wife, first and fore-most, is what defines his ministry to others.

My wife had a meaningful relationship with the Lord when we met, but it didn't look like mine because of our different upbringings. Hers was more church-oriented, while mine was more one-on-one and small group-oriented. So in my immaturity and desire to lead spiritually, my ministry to her was nothing more than an attempt to make her relation-ship with God look like mine. I wound up "lording it over her," instead of loving her in a healthy and holy way. I was not communicating sacrificial love to her, so that made it very difficult for her to respect me.

As a result of this, my wife became very much opposed to my one-on-one and small group ministry. This made it extremely difficult for me to be able to open up my home to the men with whom I was ministering. My ministry became defined as one that occurred outside of the home.

Our marriage turned into a vicious cycle. My wife felt unloved; I felt disrespected for several years. However, because of my Paul's constant involvement and direction in my life, and the pain and suffering of a contentious marriage, I started to pray earnestly for God to show me how to truly love my wife. Gradually He began to open my eyes to the fact that my wife was *a precious and priceless child of God* and needed to be ministered to in a unique way, different from the way I ministered to men. God created her to be an emotional creature and she needed me to meet her on that level -- caringly, tenderly and gently.

I have heard it said that if you think you are doing something for God, but if you do not love your wife, then you really aren't doing any-thing for God. This has proved to be true in my life. By striving to love my wife in a healthy and holy manner, living in an understanding way with her, she has the freedom to become the creation that God intended her to be – hospitable, loving, caring and gracious – and now our home is being used by God to minister to others.

## Scripture references

Galatians 5:22-23b; Romans 5:3-4; Ephesians 5:22-23; Ephesians 5:25; 2 Timothy 2:7; 1 Peter 5:3; Ephesians 5:33b; 1 Peter 3:7

........................................................................

## *Questions for reflection or discussion*

........................................................................

What are your comments on this chapter?


What has been your personal experience with this topic?


Any Scriptures or principles discussed in this chapter you need to apply in your life?

# 31.
# Children
......................

*"The father of a righteous man has great joy;*
*he who has a wise son delights in him."*
Proverbs 23:24

## *Paul's perspective*

Part of the discipling of Timothy and his maturity process also involves his children, who bless him with both positive and negative experiences. Paul must model for Timothy the understanding that the children of all ages belong to the Lord, and we are in their lives to oversee them and lead them to the Lord and His wisdom. Serving as a parent can and should be a source of joy and delight for Timothy, as such an opportunity from God ought to be.

Parents need to learn from their children. Jesus said children can serve as the greatest examples of faith, blindly trusting in their parents for survival. My friend, Kevin, tells the story of asking his children if they have ever questioned whether there would be food on the table. The kids replied, "No, Dad, we never think about that." He posed a follow-up question, inquiring if they worried about the mortgage being paid. Their response was, "What is a mortgage, Dad?"

Kevin shared this story to illustrate that childlike faith is what God is looking for in us. In Matthew 18:3, Jesus said, *"unless you are converted and become as little children, you will by no means enter the Kingdom of heaven."* Growing into childlike faith is part of Timothy's maturity process, and he can see it modeled in his children's faith. Learning from children and training them is a wonderful dichotomy accomplished as we walk in Christ.

I have heard it said that God has no grandchildren, meaning that just because a parent is a follower of Christ that does not mean that their child/children automatically inherit salvation and sanctification. Children must enter into and develop their own individual relationship with Jesus. Many kids raised in Christian homes are house-trained in the ways of Christianity, but have not had their hearts changed by Jesus Christ. When they leave the home and go away to college, entering into marriage and the workplace, their behavior and decisions often reveal their lack of a genuine commitment to follow Christ and His teachings. On the positive side, they have heard the message and in due time should develop their own relationship with Jesus.

Two things I encourage Timothy to have with his children are patience and a sense of humor. Patience is necessary because God is in control, not the parents. We must trust that He is leading His children down a path to Him and requires us to be a reflection of His unconditional love. We must also demonstrate our unwavering commitment to Christ for the kids to observe. Children ultimately walk up "fool's hill," and will make many foolish decisions and experience troubles of all kinds.

During these times, a sense of humor is of utmost importance. Timothy's frustrations and anger with the process of learning from one's mistakes are often blown way out of proportion when the parent takes the child's mistakes personally. Learning to laugh at most of their foolishness and its consequences helps children understand you are willing to trust them to the Lord. Although you are able to see the humor in their foolishness, you are still willing to let them fail. Tough love requires that parents allow their offspring to experience the consequences of their behavior, then pick them up when they fall and love them.

Some degree of conflict between Timothy and his wife over how the children will be raised is to be expected. They both come into this process with different personalities, different backgrounds and parenting experiences. Inevitably some of this will clash. This chaos is an opportunity to work through the husband/wife relationship as discussed in the chapters on "Wife" and "Leadership in the Home."

Raising children should be a focus of much prayer, along with open discussions between Timothy and his wife. It is important to have an experienced, spiritually mature couple providing counsel with the parenting process. Many mistakes can be avoided with guidance and insight provided by wise counsel. Parenting is not a solo activity, but a team experience between husband, wife, and their community of like-minded, spiritual family members.

Parenting does not cease when the children leave home. The Timothy's role with his children, and eventually his grandchildren, will continue as long as he is alive. What Timothy provides will change as his offspring get older. He will need to offer protection for young children, provide money for teens, and eventually make wisdom and godly counsel available for adult children. God will always be active with the parenting process as He allows Timothy to be an overseer, while simultaneously using the same process to grow him.

The Timothy that is divorced or remarried with children will experience a lot of pain and suffering. He will need additional support and encouragement as he walks through an experience outside of God's Biblical plan for his life. Fortunately, God does not abandon or forsake divorced Timothys. God walks through every experience with him, blessing him even (and often most especially) in the midst of suffering and chaos. If Timothy is considering or involved in the divorce process, he needs my encouragement to fight for his family and marriage. Divorce, by its very nature, brings many complicated relationship difficulties. I believe this is one practical reason that Jesus discourages divorce, although there are other reasons as well.

It is a fact that children want their family to stay intact. Children view divorce as a signal that the parent considers their needs more important than the family. Dysfunctional and rebellious behavior that ensues in children of divorce is usually a result of the loss of family. Many children think their parents have lost their right to parent them because they have abandoned the family. Divorce is not the Biblical plan for children, so I encourage Timothy to remain married, if at all possible.

When a child's parents are divorced, the offspring often feel responsible for the divorce, incurring guilt that can plague them and linger with them into adulthood. Carrying the pain of the people involved, they need to be delivered from the hurt brought about by these circumstances. If Timothy is a child of divorce, I will pray with him for his healing, whether he recognizes or admits the need for it or not.

Another situation common in our culture is that of parents wanting and attempting to be a friend to their children. As a result, a five-year-old can be entrusted with making decisions for the family. This usually doesn't make for a very pretty picture. As the children grow older, parents then try to regain control, causing a battle of the wills. As I advise my Timothy, I am not called to be my child's friend. I am called to be a parent, an authority figure, an overseer and protector.

Just as potentially detrimental to the development of children is when parents put them up on a pedestal. In a sense the children are placed on an altar, being worshiped by their parents. As these adored and idolized children grow into their teen years and later years, parents will be disappointed with their imperfections. This becomes a source of hurt, followed by painful parent-child conflicts.

Another word of counsel I offer to Timothys is the value of helping their sons as young men, once they are out of school, to get away from home and began learning to take care of themselves. This prepares them to become an overseer of a family when they find a wife. Daughters are a different story; I counsel it is best that they stay in the home as young women until married and then, with their husband, establish their own home.

Children must trustingly be given back over to God, the One who created them and loves them. As good stewards of God's children, parents need to be obedient to train them in the way they should go. And pray that they will return to His ways in which we have trained them.

## Timothy's story

My children are a gift from God, but I have not always felt that way. My wife's first marriage ended in divorce, so her two boys came with her when we married. Over the years, my wife and I have had some very difficult circumstances with them. We have dealt with issues such as shoplifting, drugs, juvenile detention, a psychiatric hospital, and even calling police to our home. On one occasion my wife and I drove three hours to pick up our 24-year-old son who was struggling with an alcohol and drug problem. Fortunately, a cab driver was willing to babysit our son at $22.50 an hour until we arrived. I felt angry, frustrated and hopeless. Additionally, I felt sorry for myself. Why did I have to rescue my adult son? Why wouldn't he grow up? Honestly, I felt like a failure as a parent, and did not know what to do.

Experts in our society tell me that if I simply had exerted more power and more control over my son, these problems would not have occurred –

or if I spent more money on counseling or treatment, the problems could have been fixed. God says in Romans 8:28: *"all things work together for good for those who love the Lord, for those who are called according to His purpose."* This has been a verse that provided hope for me with the boys.

On several occasions my Paul told me that nothing was going to change until my wife and I came into agreement. He was right. My wife and I had fought over the raising of our children most of our married life. She believed I was too hard on our children. I believed she was too soft, not allowing them to suffer consequences for their actions.

Our lack of agreement came to a head when I moved out of our home and separated from my wife, telling her I would move back in when our son moved out. He had chosen not to work or to go to school for approximately a year and a half. Instead, he occupied himself by partying with his friends, using money my wife gave him or the money that he made from selling drugs.

Fortunately, my wife had a high opinion of my Paul and another godly man that spent time with the two of us on many occasions. Through meeting with this other godly man, my Paul's Paul, we shared our hurts and our concerns, listened to his counsel, and came up with a solution. We were finally in agreement. The counsel of these other godly men softened my heart toward helping my son to get into an apartment, getting him started on a path with a good chance for living successfully on his own. This enabled my wife and me to get back together.

Although my Paul and I completed the formal *Operation Timothy* materials many years ago, I have never outgrown my need for the counsel and prayer from him. He encourages me, and helps me maintain or regain a proper perspective on many of life's challenges.

### Scripture references

Proverbs 23:24; Mark 10:15; Matthew 5:32; Proverbs 22:6; Proverbs 15:22; Joshua 1:9; Romans 8:28

......................................................................

## *Questions for reflection or discussion*

......................................................................

What are your comments on this chapter?

What has been your personal experience with this topic?

Any Scriptures or principles discussed in this chapter you need to apply in your life?

# 32.
# Spiritual Family

*"A new command I give you: Love one another. As I have loved you, so you must love one another. By this all men will know that you are my disciples, if you love one another."*
*John 13:34-35*

### Paul's perspective

The book of Genesis is the story of God's love working in mankind through various men and their families: Adam, Noah, Abraham. Abraham's family of Isaac, Jacob, and their children illustrate how important the family unit is in their relationship with each other, and with God.

In the New Testament, when Jesus began His ministry, He invested most of His time in the disciples, who made up the core of His earthly spiritual family. Since the disciples were Jesus' spiritual family, He wanted to be with them. Likewise, the apostle Paul developed his spiritual family with those he met and with disciples in various cities where he lived during his ministry.

Jesus and Paul lived their lives in front of their disciples. It is here the life of God is revealed to people who will reveal God to the next generation. Their ministries, Paul's in particular as detailed in the book of Acts, are not in the temple but in people's houses, taking place among their families.

Jesus had his human needs met in the homes of his friends. We can see the family warmth, hospitality, truth, love, and friendly conversation He engaged in during His visits to the home of Mary and Martha. He stopped by to see them not too long before going to the cross. He knew what was ahead for Him and understandably felt lonely, wanting someone to listen to Him. His human need was met as He visited in the home of these women.

The Gospel brought people into Paul's spiritual family and they became followers of Jesus. In his writings we see Paul as the overseer, instructor, and spiritual father with these followers of Jesus, who stood at the core of his own spiritual family.

In today's culture, the dysfunctional family is all too common. The love and nurturing God intended the family to provide is lacking in many troubled homes. In the past, the local church often provided the stable family for believers; in many instances, it still does. However, these days many men are failing in their attempts to have their relationship needs met through their genetic families. I've seen this over and over. When I get close enough to my Timothys, a lot of pain, sorrow, emptiness and troubles in their genetic families become evident.

Understanding the difference between genetic and spiritual family relationships is important. The genetic family is made up of people at all levels of spiritual awareness, ranging from ardent atheists to healthy functioning followers of Christ. When I am in the presence of the genetic family, it is usually more of an outreach situation where I am careful to cultivate the relationship at their personal point of spiritual maturity, worldview and needs. The genetic family is God's means for reaching men and getting the wives and kids involved is His plan. It is here husbands learn to love their wives, wives learn to respect their husbands, and together they raise their children in an understanding way. All too often, unfortunately, divorce and dysfunctional families interrupt God's plan.

When a person becomes a follower of Jesus, he comes into the spiritual family as a child needing understanding in how to live and function effectively within a family setting. This person needs a spiritual father, mother, brothers and sisters to demonstrate the life of Jesus and how to live in the family as a follower of Jesus. The spiritual family is made of like-minded followers of Christ. We also have problems, but we can deal with these problems by looking to God to guide our steps. Together we encourage and support each other in a healthy, prayerful way. Our focus is on God and His call on our lives, which ultimately is to reach the lost. That focus lies at the heart of our relationships.

For me, my spiritual family support group is made up of Timothys and like-minded believers, with whom I often co-labor in one-on-one discipleship. The men and women of my spiritual family are a group of people I can be accountable to, and they can provide a healthier, less dysfunctional, loving, spiritual family.

As I have discipled others, they have become like family to me. They connect with those in the movement who are like-minded with us about Jesus and discipleship. This spiritual family creates a lot of synergy and is very helpful, as only a family of committed believers can be.

Much of my ministry takes place in our home with my family members and those we are involved with, such as friends, neighbors and Timothys. It is in this setting the dynamics of family are revealed. God works through the little things, seen and unseen, that happen in a home between family members.

When we bring people and ministry into our home, things begin to get real at a most basic level. Activity revolves around food, fellowship and conversation. People meet our most basic needs such as love, affection, appreciation, respect and security, to name a few. It is in my home, with my spiritual and genetic family, where God becomes more than a concept or a religious preference. He becomes a way of life, being lived out in front of each other.

God has instructed man to bring Him into the home, and yet some religious people compartmentalize their lives. They keep business at the job, family in the home, and confine God to church on Sundays. They miss out on the part of one's walk with God experienced with the spiritual family in the home.

A characteristic of the JPT (Jesus, Paul, Timothy) movement is the spiritual family as a medium through which people experience the life of God in each other. With ministry in the family, we have the opportunity to see the Gospel at work. As this work results in changed lives, the validation of Jesus as the hope and glory for our lives is confirmed.

### Timothy's story

My genetic family is not the healthy support group I had hoped it would be. I did not grow up in what I would describe as a healthy genetic spiritual family. Mom was a church lady; Dad played golf on Sundays. I was almost 40 years old when I realized I was a spiritually dead man, uncertain God even existed. One divorce and a failing second marriage led me to examine the Scriptures. Through it I discovered I was a man of darkness, and I chose to leave that behind by becoming born again, inviting Jesus to take over my life.

The journey of my new life in Christ led me to a church, a large, vibrant congregation. I found knowledgeable Bible teachers and they began to educate me. It wasn't long before I was asked to teach an adult Sunday school class.

About this time I met my Paul through a Christian businessmen's group. I felt drawn to him. I visited his home and was impressed with the love and order that I observed in his family. My wife was drawn to his wife, and his children to mine.

One day while I was in the home of one of my religious mentors, he had an emotional meltdown over a business deal gone wrong. The closer I got to him by viewing his everyday life, the more his immaturity became evident in the areas of handling money, making decisions, and managing the important affairs of his life.

On the other hand, my Paul's life demonstrated unusual maturity in all areas of his life, way beyond my personal level of maturity in those same areas. I began to invest more and more time into this relationship with my Paul. Gradually I accepted him as my spiritual father, and his family became my spiritual family. We have been together more than 20 years, and we continue to grow together, co-laboring in the lifelong process of knowing Christ and making Him known.

One of my Paul's major contributions to me has been in enabling me to personally observe the indwelling life of Christ in him. This has occurred repeatedly while spending much time in each other's homes, with our families living out normal activities in everyday life. When I went through dark days with problems that seemed overwhelming, it was in his home that I found the comfort and closeness I so desperately needed. In these times of suffering and hardship, I experienced Christ through my Paul and our spiritual family. Today I am experiencing the fullness of Christ within myself.

Now I use my home as a place to enjoy my relationships with other people and fellowship with my spiritual family. My wife is a great asset to my discipleship ministry. She is a great cook and many people are able to enjoy her creations. We are a team and our purpose is to know Christ and make Him known.

## *Scripture references*

John 13:34-35; Psalm 90:10; Deuteronomy 6:6-7; Mark 3:14; 2 Corinthians 2:12-13; Acts; Luke 10:38-42; 1 Corinthians 4:15b; John 3:1-21; Galatians 4:19

...........................................................................

# *Questions for reflection or discussion*

...........................................................................

What are your comments on this chapter?

What has been your personal experience with this topic?

Any Scriptures or principles discussed in this chapter you need to apply in your life?

# 33.
# Work
. . . . . . . . . . . . . .

*"Do not work for food that spoils, but for*
*food that endures to eternal life.,,,"*
John 6:27

## *Paul's perspective*

Jesus tells us that we are not to work for temporal things that will perish, but to do the work He gives, which is eternal. This is a challenge for the men I have discipled because most have experienced mid-life conversions. Having spent 30 to 40 years on the wrong side of the cross, and many years laboring in the cutthroat, unforgiving marketplace, they then struggle with Jesus' command to not work for "meat that perishes."

Timothys are often comfortable with the way they have always done things, laboring to provide for themselves. Then they discover that a 180-degree change is required by Jesus. Having been street fighters with a survival mentality, turning their self-sufficiency over and exchanging it for dependence on God is a scary proposition. To have someone walk with them is virtually the only channel to educate Timothy in this new way of living.

Men tend to find identity in their work, using it to measure their perceived value and status with peers. Work often defines a man's existence, determining his overall assessment of success or failure. When I disciple a man, his marriage, family and work tend to be the major focus of his life. None of these are easy focal points, so we spend a significant amount of time in discussion and prayer regarding each area. Work in particular tends to dominate a man's time, often taking up to 60 hours a week, sometimes more than that. Marriage and family receive much smaller allocations of time. This type of schedule leaves little if any time for exercise, recreation, or spiritual matters. If he can begin to bring order into these areas, then he can find time to give to other people.

During this time of reordering and transition to a new and unfamiliar way of living, a lot of questions come up with Timothy that need answering. The question of his income and living standard is typically a major issue. Do I trust Jesus with determining how much money I will make? Can I serve both God and money?

I often lived as if I were going to prove to be the first guy that could serve both of these masters. It took a long time, frantically switching back and forth from my business hat to my God hat, but God at last convinced me I could not serve both. Finally, after much struggle, I was able to keep my "serving God hat" on all the time.

Sometimes new Timothys think they need a job or career change to effectively serve God. I usually encourage him to stay where he is in the marketplace until he learns to be content, and at that point God will sometimes move him to a new situation. He needs to learn to build relationships that lead to discipleship where he is, putting his new faith into practice in familiar surroundings, not running off to pursue some other endeavor.

Walking alongside Timothy through this often painful process of change is my job. Sometimes God even takes his work away from him, bringing his business life to a dead halt. God wants us to know that He is our provider. Providing for us when our work is taken from us is one way He teaches us to trust Him.

These are difficult lessons, so it is always great to have someone walking through the process with us. I pray with Timothy that he will have the courage to persevere through this changeover from self-dependence to God-dependence for his financial provision. Unfortunately, some men are not brave enough to take this risk and thus become stuck in a place that stymies their success in the process of becoming functional disciples and disciplemakers.

Work is an area a man must order and limit, so it doesn't become the purpose, focus and passion of his life, at the expense of everything else. The marketplace is a logical place for Timothy to find men he can befriend and eventually disciple. This gives him a new reason for going to work.

## Timothy's story

At age 40 I became a believer in Christ as my Savior and began my journey of becoming His follower. My experience of discovering Christianity and Biblical truth created in me a desire to share this truth with others. My work as a real estate broker presented many opportunities to meet people and share my enthusiasm for Christian truths. However, I had heard two things you do not discuss in business are religion and politics. I was open to using the marketplace as a forum for sharing Christ, but was reluctant to do so because I did not want to run off my clients. I had observed a few religious zealots – and I sure did not want to be like them.

When I met my Paul, he began to model a low-key approach for building relationships with men before entering into spiritual discussions and I started taking the same approach. Before long I began to feel a real tension between the time I spent working versus the time spent discipling men. Over a period of four years, I experienced financial gain and then a major failure of my business. This last failure was the third of my business career and led me to make a decision.

I had been working 40 hours or more per week, then spending additional hours discipling men. At age 44 I had given my life to work and it had yielded a big pile of nothing. I had built three businesses that all ended in failure. In one case I acted stupidly, but in the others I had been a hapless victim of major market changes that destroyed the businesses. I finally was ready to trust Christ for my level of income, even if it meant having to live a more frugal lifestyle.

Going forward, I decided to limit my workweek to 25 hours and devote 15 hours to discipling men. One of my thoughts was that most people don't really work 40 hours anyway because they are distracted and focused on outside interests. I would be very careful to dedicate an earnest five hours of work each weekday and trust God to provide.

In the ensuing years, my income was more than adequate. God provided deals yielding larger commissions, which afforded me the free time for discipling men without changing our lifestyle. The time I have devoted to discipleship has rewarded me many times over. Work is a part of my life, but now I view it only as the way I fund the ministry God has given me to do. Ministry can be work too, so I take the same approach for it as I do with business, budgeting my time in both areas and keeping a balance in my activities.

## Scripture references

John 6:27; 1 Corinthians 7:24; Matthew 6:24; 1 Corinthians 15:58

..................................................................

## Questions for reflection or discussion

..................................................................

What are your comments on this chapter?

What has been your personal experience with this topic?

Any Scriptures or principles discussed in this chapter you need to apply in your life?

# 34.
# True Community

·············································

*"The sacrifices of God are a broken spirit; a broken and
contrite heart, O God, you will not despise."*
*Psalm 51:17*

## Paul's perspective

For those followers of Christ who choose to take part in the one-on-one discipleship process and desire to experience true community, the road is one of trials and continual sifting. Growth comes as a result of suffering, brokenness, humility and forgiveness. It is good when we can have the companionship of our spiritual community as we walk through this often difficult, lifelong process.

The prayers and fellowship of our brothers will encourage us and strengthen our faith, resulting in our coming through the trials and becoming a source of strength to our brothers. The process of experiencing true community is special, but unfortunately is not experienced or understood by many who proclaim to be followers of Christ.

Over time I have observed that community comes in two forms: *pseudo-community* and *true community*. Pseudo-community can be identified as "light and polite" or superficial conversation. By comparison, true community would be conversation consisting of genuine, significant and personal exchange. For example, as a career salesman I try to find common ground with others based on my knowledge, experiences, acquaintances or other similarities. If a person says they went to Spain, I will come back with, "Oh, I was there in the '80s on the Costa del Sol in Spain. What a place." It is simple conversation where one party serves up a bit of information and the other party bats it back, much like ping-pong. These are good "ice breaking" exchanges, but are without depth, and therefore not true community.

True community is built on dialogue that continues over time, where I get to know someone and build a vulnerable, transparent relationship with them. These relationships involve discovering our differences and accepting one another in spite of those differences.

The steps of building true community are as follows:

1. Pseudo-Community
2. Chaos
3. Emptiness
4. True Community

The world teaches people to avoid chaos and emptiness. When men insist on compromise, working out win-win solutions to problems, they will not get out of pseudo-community. True community is birthed out of conflict, chaos and brokenness. To build a healthy relationship I must move from pseudo-community to chaos. To put it another way, I discover through dialogue that I don't agree with you. The more I explore my differences, the more I am separated from others by them, until I feel separation and emptiness. It is in this emptiness that I decide whether I will accept you with your differences and reconcile with you, in order to move forward in our relationship.

An example of how community works would be participating in a civic association's meeting to discuss planting trees on the neighborhood esplanade. One group wants to plant Pine Trees, but I am convinced that Live Oak Trees would be a better choice. After a lively discussion (chaos) a vote is taken and the Pine Tree group wins. I move into emptiness, thinking maybe I will call the Realtor and sell my house. I can choose to accept the reality that this will end my relationship with my neighbors. But if I accept them as being different and thinking differently, and die to my need to be right, I can enter into true community with them. So now I can choose to show up Saturday morning and help my neighbors plant the Pine Trees. (Note: Building community is illustrated in Appendix III to help you in gaining a better understanding of the community process.)

Many men avoid conflict, so modeling these steps for Timothy is critical in his process of learning to develop true community with other people. I have found that achieving true community is difficult; it involves understanding I am incapable of doing it without it being God's work. But if Timothy and I do succeed in entering into true community, the relationship deepens, grows and expands.

People of the world, including like-minded believers, largely exist in a pseudo-community where everyone is imperfect. Because I am imperfect, I must be willing to accept others' imperfections. In my experience, acceptance has been the key to building authentic relationships and moving toward true community with imperfect people. In discipleship, I spend a lot of time with Timothy and we will find differences. I must and will, in the spirit of true community, set aside the chaos, separation and emptiness that can develop because of our discovered differences. To restore the relationship, I must re-enter the relationships with forgiveness and acceptance.

Community is stimulated when people choose to stay in a relationship and love a person regardless of differences. The process encourages listening and understanding, not just getting our own way. A person seeking community will not abort the four-step process, and in so doing will develop long-term, deep relationships with others, honoring their value and giftedness.

I have discovered that in my life, I don't grow much outside of true community. For me, growth occurs when I become a servant to my Timothy. He and I are becoming a team for the cause of the Gospel. A united team effort is synonymous with community. As a team we are devoted to Christ, to the Gospel, and to one another. Because of this devotion, we set aside our differences, enter into true community, and press on in the calling of disciplemaking.

In addition to working through our differences, walking with my disciples through the trials of life becomes a major part of building community with them. Community develops when people are sifted, as if poured through a filter that eliminates impurities and extraneous material. Those that stick with me, through my trials and their own, are the ones that become lifetime authentic friends. It is in the fire of these trials that we learn to love each other properly, and then become freed up and able to be more pleasing to God.

### Timothy's story

When my daughter was a preteen, I signed her up for a girls' basketball team in the local area kids' sports association and agreed to coach the team. My daughter had played on a couple of softball teams, but had no basketball experience. My Timothy's daughter had played on some basketball teams and he had coached those teams. I invited them to join the team, and he agreed to be my assistant coach. I thought this would be an opportunity for the four of us to get to know each other in a competitive environment.

We were in a league that played at a local junior high school gym. The league lasted about four months, including preseason practice and a season-ending championship tournament.

As we got into the preseason practices, my goal for the team was that the girls would enjoy the team experience, have a good time, and end up liking basketball – and each other. My Timothy is a very competitive guy with considerable basketball experience, both in teaching and playing. His goal, however, was to win every game, regardless of how these little girls felt, and be the league champion at the end of the season.

Our two different agendas began to fly in the face of each other as we started putting the team together. We got into a lot of chaos with the girls and each other over the course of the season.

At the end of the season our team was in the finals of the championship game. My Timothy's daughter, the star player on the team, injured her knee and as a result we lost the final game.

Despite the conflict, the whole experience turned out for the good with my Timothy and our relationship. We realized that we were two very different people with different goals and different ways, but we had stayed in the process and worked it through until we achieved community. We accepted each other's roles and our different styles with the girls. I took the part more of the team-builder side of the process; and he addressed more the aspect of the game's competiveness, the drills and game strategies. So we functioned properly as a team.

It's been 25 years since we had that experience and our daughters are still friends. Timothy and I are still co-laboring in the life-on-life discipleship ministry and remain close friends. We don't have to avoid chaos with each other, as we have learned that true community is easy for us to achieve.

We realized that my giftedness is that of a team builder while he is a directive leader. When these two types of personalities get together and don't understand each other, a lot of fireworks can take place. Fortunately, we understood that we were learning what true community is all about.

As we worked through the many situations that involved chaos and emptiness, we were able get to community over the four-month season many times. We stayed the course and learned through the process. Today we realize our story offers a strong example of how relationships can be strengthened and matured when individuals understand and are willing to remain in the relationship and work toward true community.

## Scripture references
Psalm 51:17; Mark 10:43-44; Luke 10:38-42; Luke 22:24-34; John 19:26-27; Romans 5:3-4

........................................................................

# Questions for reflection or discussion
........................................................................

What are your comments on this chapter?

What has been your personal experience with this topic?

Any Scriptures or principles discussed in this chapter you need to apply in your life?

# 35.
# Leadership in the Home

······················································

*"However, each one of you also must love his wife as he loves*
*himself, and the wife must respect her husband."*
Ephesians 5:33

## *Paul's perspective*

Just as Christ gave Himself up for us, a husband must give up some of his agenda to serve his family. Each man has his own success-oriented agenda he plans on accomplishing. Business, recreation, sports, and various projects would head the list of things men might put ahead of their family. Perhaps with this in mind, the apostle Paul in his letter to the Ephesians instructs the husband to take responsibility for the leadership of his home. This does not mean the husband is more important than the wife, but I believe this means he has the role of presenting Jesus Christ to his wife, modeling before her a healthy relationship with our Lord, hopefully becoming a life she can follow.

My role with Timothy is to encourage him to learn to listen to his wife and respond to her needs. To do this effectively, I must demonstrate this for him. Sharing my own failures and successes in this area is critical to this modeling process. Bringing Timothy into my home where he can witness my marriage relationship is also necessary, as that is where he can see what this really looks like. If he comes often enough he will see the real, actual version of our marriage and not some staged, unrealistic version.

Leadership in the home began for me by learning to listen to my wife. It is a lesson I have had to learn the hard way. In the past I have made important decisions without her counsel, which hurt her because I was not conveying that her opinions mattered. I've learned that God speaks to me through my wife – when I listen to her. There was a time when I took the caveman approach, pulling her in the direction I wanted to go. This caused problems as my one-sided decisions often proved to be unwise. My wife became critical of me and lost respect for me. I can make decisions, but when I humble myself and involve her, many times God has used her to reveal His will. I believe the Bible clearly calls men to be the spiritual overseers in their homes. God desires to speak to the man about his family and have him respond by overseeing his family spiritually with love and humility. The man should determine, first by considering his wife's spiritual needs, how his family will follow the Lord. This could include Bible reading and study, prayer, church attendance, home church, one-on-one discipleship, missionary work, even neighborhood ministry.

Spiritual leadership in the home, coupled with learning to live with a woman in an understanding way, are critical commands for married men. Many males find this to be the most difficult challenge they face in life. Unfortunately, men often do not function as leaders, nor are they respected in their home; instead, they are being led by their wives. When a man fails to lead, it is not uncommon for the wife to take over that role, whether she wants it or not.

When the wife leads in spiritual matters, all too often the man turns into a spiritual wimp. Women do not respect wimpy men, and respect is the major need for a man in the marriage relationship. A wife's decision to respect her husband should come from a conviction based on the Scriptures concerning her responsibility to respect him. In reality, however, her respect typically will be earned by the husband being trustworthy. Ultimately, God intended the man to take the responsibility of becoming the spiritual leader of the family – and it is up to him to be faithful to that calling.

Wives may be responsible in other areas, such as child nurturing, hospitality, decorating, and cleanliness. A wife might be an accountant or an expert in the financial field, so it might make sense for her to take the responsibility in that area – but the husband must not abandon his responsibility to know what is going on. My wife and I have regular meetings, usually the same time each week, to discuss our busy lives. It is in these meetings – we call them "staff meetings" – that I seek her counsel on the important aspects and decisions of our family and the business.

Husbands need to take the lead in bringing order to their homes, and money is a common root of disorder and chaos in families. The control of spending is a function of budgeting. If the man will take the lead in this, or any other area, it is then up to the wife to decide to follow. Eventually this leads to the wife yielding to the man's leadership role in decision-making. In this way, she is not simply trusting her man but also learning to trust the Lord, knowing her husband is responsible to God for the decisions he makes in leading the family. Thus she learns to yield her will in accepting God's plan for her role in the marriage.

This issue comes down to the wife giving respect to her husband by submitting to his lead. No one can make another person submit, or for that matter, cause anyone to change. It sometimes takes a few years, with the husband attempting to lead and demonstrating to her the love of Christ, before the wife begins to respond. These can be difficult years for Timothy and he will need my prayer and encouragement in his endeavors to gain the spiritual leadership of his home.

Most women want and need a man who lives out his God-given responsibility to lead his family. Over time as she sees him following Christ, and feels loved as she needs to be loved, she will begin to respect him and follow his leadership. Men need to be respected as much as wives need to be loved if the marriage is to be a healthy one. The wife's respect will grow out of the husband's willingness to speak the truth in love to her, as he graciously listens and shows he is equally willing to learn from her.

## Timothy's story

My Paul and I were standing in line at a cafeteria when he turned to me and said, "You know, your wife wears the pants in your family, and God wants you to step up and be the leader." Wow, that was a hard statement to hear from someone I respected so much. I was glad he was speaking the truth to me in the hope that I would grow up in Christ with respect to my role as a leader in my own home.

The typical scenario in our family dynamic was that when we had problems with our young teenage daughter, I would defer the decision to my wife even though I didn't necessarily agree with her. I would stuff my feelings inside, rather than dealing with any kind of chaos that might result. Periodically a big issue would arise and I would explode in anger.

Such behavior would serve only to unite my wife and my daughter, driving a wedge between my wife and me.

After my Paul made his observation, I decided to begin to move – in God's power – into the leadership role. One piece of counsel we got from my Paul and his wife, who also was discipling my wife, was that we shouldn't make any decisions regarding our daughter until we prayed together and got into complete agreement over the matter. That principle was probably the most important one we learned, both for dealing with our daughter and for any other decisions we have had to make.

I wish I could say God changed me overnight to be the leader of the family, but He didn't. Old habits die hard, but my wife was able to observe my attempts to lead our family as the husband and father God would want me to be. She gradually submitted to me as I earned her respect and the right to lead. I've learned the wife will fill the leadership gap if the husband fails to do so because she doesn't want to see the family fail, but she also has an instinctive desire to be led by her husband.

After a number of years, I did become the leader of our family. It was affirmed to me one day when my daughter called asking for something. I said, "I don't know, have you asked your mom about it?" She replied, "Dad, she will just say you're the father and I will have to discuss it with you." This showed me that we finally were all on the same page as a family, trying to deal with issues the right way – on God's terms.

### Scripture references

Ephesians 5:25-33; Ephesians; 4:15; Philippians 4:13; Philippians 3:12-14

...............................................................

## *Questions for reflection or discussion*

...............................................................

What are your comments on this chapter?

What has been your personal experience with this topic?

Any Scriptures or principles discussed in this chapter you need to apply in your life?

# 36.
# Order

................

*"But everything should be done in a fitting and orderly way."*
*1 Corinthians 14:40*

## Paul's perspective

Without order it is very difficult to lead a mature life because we
are constantly distracted by chaos. As men mature in Christ, one of the
godly traits they begin to focus on is having an ordered life. Jesus promises us peace and rest if we come to Him, and it is important for Paul to
realize that Timothy needs a role model to imitate and follow.

Paul is not perfect, but he has walked with Jesus Christ long enough
that he is living a life that makes sense. This is the model Timothy has
been searching for. As Timothy orders his life, he will begin to mature
in competency, character, and eventually community with Paul and like-
minded men.

Order comes out of simplicity, making choices to have and to do less.
Fewer commitments and less spending are examples of simplification.
Bondage to preferences only complicates life. Preferences might include:
insisting on a new car, convinced that a used one won't do; continuing
a quest to live in "the neighborhood"; or determining that only special
clothing labels will satisfy. Modeling simplicity for Timothy, along with
my trust that God is interested in every circumstance of my life, helps
him to do likewise. Sharing little stories of my life choices helps both of
us to become ordered and stay that way.

Timothy and I live in a fast-paced, complex world where chaos and
disorder dominate the lives of many men. There are reasons for the dysfunctional, chaotic circumstances exhibited in each man's life, and the
situations surrounding these problems are unique with each individual.

Our spiritual enemy understands this and utilizes chaos and disorder to take men out of ordered lives that God could use for His glory.

Among the major causes of disorder are money management, time management, relationships, immaturity, and unhealthy lifestyles. There are others, but all are reflective of poor self-management and failure to set priorities. Greediness – wanting way more than we need or can afford – seems to be at the root of most unhealthy lifestyle choices.

I find that even as men realize chaos is ruling their lives, they tend to resist order, choosing to embrace a crisis management lifestyle. Or they become desperate for peace and change, but find themselves ill-equipped and powerless to make the necessary changes. Where should we start in this process? With such an overwhelming task, I believe you must decide to bring order to one thing at a time. It's no different than how you would eat a whale: Just one bite at a time. The first area that needs to be ordered is the spiritual life. This involves putting Jesus on the throne, committing to be obedient to His commands, getting into His Word, praying often, having fellowship with like-minded followers of Christ, and effectively sharing your faith with others.

As Timothy and I identify areas of his life that are causing him disorder and chaos, we begin to pray. If a man has a plan to simplify and bring order, if asked, God will guide his steps. We find the path the Lord leads a man down is usually not the way we would choose to go, but He knows best how to bring about permanent changes that will lead to a new way of living, one that is ordered and manageable.

The basic steps to eliminate chaos are:

1. Identify the cause or root of the chaos.
2. Adopt simplicity in that area, which will result in order if the power of God is leading.

As order is achieved, the peace resulting from the elimination of chaos will stimulate the desire to identify the purpose for one's life. Then one can begin setting goals leading to a life full of purpose and true meaning. Purpose allows a man to set priorities and make wise choices.

This process takes time, anywhere from five to twenty years or more, depending on the individual person. As Timothy must be patient, I also must be patient and walk with him through this difficult time of transition. For me, the discipleship process is a lifelong commitment to Timothy. Prayer time together, God's modeling through my life, observing changes in his life, and my encouragement throughout all serve to drive the process of bringing order into his life as the three of us (JPT) walk down life's road together. We are encouraged to imitate Paul and strive for the perfection we see in our Heavenly Father. The result we seek is an ordered, simplified life that Jesus can use for God's glory.

## *Timothy's story*

There was a point in my younger life when I found myself without a home. I was sleeping in my car at the end of a street. I had moved out of the house I'd shared with the mother of my newborn son, leaving everything except a laundry basket of dirty clothes that I took with me. There was an embankment that came down to a stream. The first night there, I stood on the embankment looking down at the stream that had been trashed and polluted with tires, empty bottles and tin cans. Observing this mess, I had the revelation that this was similar to what my life looked like, trashed and polluted because of total chaos and poor decisions. I stayed there a couple of nights in the car, knowing it would be a long time before I would see my son again.

With no place left to go, I moved back into my mother's home and slept on her laundry room floor. One night as I was reflecting on the little pieces of my shattered life, I noticed my childhood Bible sitting on the bottom of some shelving. It reminded me of God and my need for a higher purpose for my life. I began to pray, asking God to let me see my son again and resolving, if He would, I would commit to grow up and become the man He wanted me to be.

I began taking logical steps that produced some good results. I went back to school and began to prioritize studying, getting rest, and working. Eventually I initiated a custody battle with my son's mother. Piecing my life together brought about positive developments, including my school grades. Eventually I obtained primary custody of my son.

It has been eight years since I began striving to live an ordered life, going to school and focusing on accepting my parental responsibilities. During this time I began to meet with my Paul. My formal spiritual growth took off as I spent time with him and studied the Scriptures. I was learning what God's plan for my life was and what it should look like. I began to see that Jesus Christ was truly interested in every detail of my everyday life.

Through the discipleship process I was introduced to new concepts previously unknown to me. First and foremost was the concept of "margin." Margin is the excess "space" available after tasks and responsibilities are complete. Margin can pertain to energy, time, money, or other personal resources. As I matured in Christ through the discipleship process, it became clear that lack of order was the cause of the chaotic, no-margin life I was living.

Through years of meeting with and watching Paul, I began to see a new way of living. The distractions and noise of our world didn't take hold and dominate Paul's life. Paul modeled this for me by turning his cell phone off during our meetings and time together. This was the first time I ever noticed someone drawing a line in the sand and shutting the world's noise out when it was interfering with an established priority.

Through Paul, I have learned to rest in the fact that God is ultimately in control of all things. Everything belongs to Him. Riches, honor, power and might come from Him and it is at His discretion that I am made great and given strength. This teaches me that no matter how hard I try, no matter how many phone calls I answer, no matter how many tasks I complete, it is in God's hand whether I succeed or fail.

This truth began to sink into my mind and heart. Over a period of five years I met my wife and got married. We became a blended family and there is a lot of chaos, but with God in our lives and at the center of our home, there was a much bigger sense of purpose. We then came to a place where we wanted to have a fourth child together, desiring to complete our family.

I was at a point where I was able to look at our home and make some physical changes that would bring more order to our family life. We stepped back and prioritized family time. We began organizing our home to make room for this newborn baby. We expanded and finished our attic, created more storage space, moved two kids upstairs and furnished a nursery for our soon-to-be-born son.

Because of my growth spiritually, I was able to prioritize and look at what was needed. That would not have been possible for me eight to ten years earlier. As I had grown spiritually, I gained an understanding of the need for order in my life and how it could be achieved.

Currently we have four children. My wife and I have been married five years and have a new son that is 12 weeks old. My wife and I recently revisited that dead-end street where I had once lived. I told her about where I had come from, wanting to use the stream as an illustration. But when we parked and went to look at the creek, it had been cleaned up. All the trash was gone. It had been turned into a very pretty little stream. As I looked and thought about this, I realized that like the stream, my once-polluted life had become ordered, restored and cleaned up.

### Scripture references

Matthew 11:28-30; 1 Corinthians 14:40; Proverbs 16:9; Matthew 5:48; 1 Corinthians 4:16; 1 Chronicles 29:11-12; Matthew 10:29-31; 1 John 5:14;

. . . . . . . . . . . . . . . . . . . . . . . . . . . . . . . . . . . . . . . . . . . . . . . . . . . . . . . . . . . . . . . . . .

## Questions for reflection or discussion

. . . . . . . . . . . . . . . . . . . . . . . . . . . . . . . . . . . . . . . . . . . . . . . . . . . . . . . . . . . . . . . . . .

What are your comments on this chapter?

What has been your personal experience with this topic?

Any Scriptures or principles discussed in this chapter you need to apply in your life?

# 37.
# Stewardship

........................................

*"No one can serve two masters. He will hate the one and love the other, or he will be devoted to the one and despise the other. You cannot serve both God and money."*
*Matthew 6:24*

## Paul's perspective

It is best for Timothys to order their lives to be more available to God. Failure to be orderly in the use of the resources God entrusts a man to manage while on this planet is a source of disorder. These resources include our body, wife, family, the environment, money, and everything that money buys. In the Bible, love is mentioned over 400 times and prayer 155 times. But our hearts can so easily become money-centered, and God is well aware of how it competes with a Christ-focused relationship. So He has spoken about money more than 2,300 times in the Scriptures. With that amount of emphasis, I believe the stewardship of money is of great importance to God.

Openness with Timothy in the area of stewardship is very important to our relationship. When Timothy broaches the subject of financial issues, it pleases me because I view it as a statement of his level of trust with me. Usually he will begin to expose his money matters when I openly discuss mine. Initiating the process is as simple as telling him how I handle money and budgeting. I do not hesitate to discuss and reveal personal finances, including facts and figures. If I am reluctant, Timothy may also be reluctant to be open about this area of his life.

By talking candidly about financial matters, Timothy views me as a safe person he can trust with a subject many men consider very personal and hold very private. I begin these delicate discussions by mentioning that everything belongs to God, pointing out "our" money does not belong to us. He entrusts us with these material blessings to have, hold and manage as His stewards – as He sees fit – in a manner and for a time He determines. Once Timothy understands this, he can begin to make progress in the ordering of his finances. It is not uncommon for men of all ages to have major financial problems, largely because they have failed to be good stewards of God's possessions in not following God's financial advice as plainly communicated in the Scriptures.

Money problems are a major cause of divorces. Emotional conflict often finds its root in poor financial stewardship and the ensuing consequences. At some point I ask Timothy and his wife, if he has one, to participate in what is called a *Crown Study*. Crown Financial Ministries offers this excellent study detailing what God has to say about money and proper stewardship.

The vicious cycle of spending more than you earn, then borrowing to cover the shortfall, is common in our society. It's even modeled by our nation's government. The "I want what I want, and I want it right now" mindset has thrust a majority of our culture into bondage, making them slaves to their lenders. The financial fallout created in just a few years of overspending can take a decade or longer to remedy. Once Timothy makes a decision to live on what he makes and to stop borrowing, the healing process can begin. The goal is to be personally debt-free, with adequate reserves in the bank. There also may be the entirely different matter of business debt we might need to deal with, but whether the finances are for personal or business use, the sound, Biblical principles of stewardship are the same.

Teaching men to give money is another aspect of stewardship we need to address. I learned to give joyfully because my Paul led me in becoming a giver. A couple of years after we began meeting, my Paul instructed me to bring my checkbook to the next meeting. Then he asked me to write a check for $100. I filled the check out. He then asked me to make it out to the local ministry we both were involved with, explaining how I needed to support the full-time leadership men.

Not being a giver, I wasn't very happy about doling out my dollars. My Paul further frustrated me when he said I would be receiving an envelope monthly and he expected me to give 100 smackers every time. "Every month?" I responded, questioning his meaning. His reply was hard-hitting and straightforward. "I see how you live, what you spend, where you live, the car you drive, and you can afford to give $100."

Each month, I received the envelope in the mail and my hand would shake as I wrote out the check. This was very contrary to my mindset of "Get all you can, can all you get." I had become accustomed to hoarding money, keeping everything I made for myself. This was diametrically opposed to what was being asked and expected of me, venturing into a whole new way of living and managing what was not mine but God's. When I look back, little by little with the passing of each month, it became easier to write the check. By letting go through giving, I was releasing my tight-fistedness, my grasp on money and love for it. After a while it became fun to write the check. Then, after a little more time passed, the fun in making the monthly gift became a joy.

This was the manner in which God helped me to release my hold on money and its hold over me. It was such a tremendous thing and I am so happy this man, my Paul, did this for me – because it changed my life. He was certain it would, and that was the reason he gave me the lesson in giving. He was a guy willing to go out on the edge, tell me what I needed to do, and make sure I did it.

Helping Timothy to give, and through it to support the work of discipleship and evangelism, is another topic for discussion. If he is married, the use of money to support such endeavors can be sticky process between the couple. Developing a budget and learning to live within its boundaries is a crucial part of stewardship maturity. No one has unlimited resources, so we all must make choices on where and how we spend God's money. Over time these money matters can be addressed and eventually Timothy will be able to take stewardship responsibility of all other resources God has given him.

### Timothy's story

I became a follower of Jesus Christ in 1998 while being discipled by another man. My issue with money has been not having enough of it, getting into debt, and then trying to wiggle my way out. I have my own business and work in sales. Because of this my income always fluctuates. I have had times when I had lots of money and times when I had none. This is tough for any man, but especially difficult when he's married, with four children and a wife that didn't work outside the home for several years while the children were young.

I became awakened to my own financial situation when I counseled a man who was $100,000 in debt. He began taking over the management of their finances from his wife and dealing with the creditors. I watched as God began providing the means for him to pay off much of the debt.

This situation served to bring me back to my own financial problems. I was $45,000 in debt, excluding our mortgage. The difficult part was managing our many medical, dental, school and sports expenses while having a variable income. My wife was handling our finances, which was unfair because she did not know when – or if – money was coming in. Our communication was poor at best, and at the time I was happy to just ignore the entire situation.

Our financial situation was difficult. I saw so much good in the Lord, but had things so messed up I couldn't see why or how He would care for my needs. I wanted freedom from the cursed dead life I led, but didn't know how to achieve it. I really wanted to step up and do what was necessary, but it scared me to death.

I am not the smartest guy, and why God chose me is beyond me, but Christ did free me and provided a path to freedom and away from the world and its traps. I understood I had received immediate restoration through Christ Jesus, but my problems were not immediately resolved. I finally came to realize these were no longer my problems to solve. God would bring the solutions as I remained faithful and followed His instructions.

My problems were covered by the promise that God had made to me and now they were just leftovers of a fallen life for which I was responsible. Once I began to pray and get seriously committed to paying off our debt, God provided the income for doing that much faster than I had imagined. I met with other men who had been in similar situations, prayed about it, mapped out a plan for getting out of debt, and then handed it over to God, trusting Him to take care of the details.

This combination of variable income and increased expenses has deepened my faith and dependence on God as I trust Him to provide. I changed my ways too, making repairs when I was able, instead of calling on and paying for repairmen. We take our time in making purchase decisions now and pray about entering into financial commitments. I have consistently made efforts not to make lengthy loans requiring payments over extended periods of time. This has decreased our monthly expenses and given me the freedom to survive financially during the lean months when our income is low.

I stayed fairly consistent in God's Word and prayer during this time. Therefore, I believe the Holy Spirit prompts and clues me in to situations or actions I need to take. I also seek the counsel of several different people and consider various options when encountering a problem. Once information is gathered, I then pray about it and wait for God's guidance, direction and answer. I learned this from my Paul and believe God approves of this process. This is what good stewardship looks like to me.

I still make some mistakes, but God has continued to allow me to manage our finances and provide situations I can learn from. The things of God are beyond me, and He can only begin working on me, through me, and in me when I give up control. For His power to take charge, my struggle over my will and desire to control must end.

Making some of the decisions on my finances was not easy and at times has required leaps of faith, but God has always come through for me and blessed it. I can't believe it, but I actually have joy in handling the finances, whereas before I didn't. Being in debt and getting out of it has been a blessing. I have been told this was an opportunity to move closer to God and watch Him work out the details, one by one. And that has truly been the case.

God has moved me closer to His Kingdom. Looking back, this process has actually been a lot easier than I imagined. I know it is all God, protecting and providing for me. As I am learning to stand up and be a man in this arena, God is faithful.

## *Scripture references*

Matthew 6:24; Proverbs 22:7; 2 Corinthians 9:6-7; 1 John 2:15-16; Ephesians 4:4-6

## *Questions for reflection or discussion*

What are your comments on this chapter?

What has been your personal experience with this topic?

Any Scriptures or principles discussed in this chapter you need to apply in your life?

# 38.
# Testimony

......................

*"And this is the testimony: God has given us eternal life, and*
*this life is in his Son. He who has the Son has life; he who does*
*not have the Son of God does not have life. I write these*
*things to you who believe in the name of the Son of*
*God so that you may know that you have eternal life."*
*1 John 5:11-13*

## Paul's perspective

When I meet a potential Timothy, one of my goals is at some point to share with him my personal testimony about Jesus Christ and His impact on my life. Part of this involves waiting for a time when circumstances open the door to share portions or all of my testimony. Once the door opens, I share my story (or parts of it) so Timothy can begin to share his story, if he has one, with me. His story may start with an experience of praying for Jesus to come into his life as a child or teenager. Or he might have had a conversion experience at a religious event or service at another time in his life.

Some men have no story to share. Determining where Timothy is in his life with Christ as his Savior and as his Lord is a critical part of my relationship with him. I am praying for his relationship with Christ to grow and mature. This relationship is at the heart of his testimony, which he will be able to share with others the rest of his life.

I find that Christians have many varied ideas regarding the word "testimony." Let me begin by clarifying my definition of the word. By *testimony,* I am referring to an individual's personal story regarding how and why Christ came to be the most important relationship in their lives. To be effective in the presentation of this story, a well-written account is extremely helpful. My job is to walk Timothy through the writing of his testimony.

A testimony has several key elements: early life before accepting Christ; the steps that led up to conversion; the conversion experience, and the difference having a relationship with Christ has made in one's life. At the testimony's foundation is recognizing the need for Christ in our lives. We need Him because of our sinful nature, which separates us from God. If Timothy recognizes he is a sinner, this need is obvious to him (Romans 3:23 and 6:23). If he sees himself as a good guy, the need may be hard for him to grasp. Regardless of where he is, the need for Christ as his Savior, to experience reconciliation to God, is a necessary and central part of a man's testimony (1 Corinthians 15:1-5).

Another element of one's testimony is that we are changed by the life of Christ in us. While the first part is our assurance that we will not go to hell but to heaven when we die, the second part speaks to Christ coming out of heaven to live in us (Galatians 2:20). In essence, this is the story of God's Kingdom becoming a part of us (Matthew 6:9-10). We become a walking, talking advertisement for Kingdom living and thinking that has taken over our life. Timothy's ability to grasp and communicate his Kingdom testimony will be used by God with others he disciples and with whom he builds relationships.

Jesus had a great deal to say about the Kingdom. (See Appendix II for more of what He said.) The word "Kingdom" appears 121 times in the four Gospels, while the word "church" appears only three times. Jesus modeled for the disciples a loving, humble, gentle, honest nature. He was not impressed by worldly accomplishments centered on position, power and prestige.

As a believer, Timothy is now a member of God's Kingdom and living in Jesus' presence. Grasping that he is now in the Kingdom is difficult for many because it is invisible, yet real. My Paul offered an interesting analogy when he told me about his five-year-old granddaughter. She has a Japanese father, and with her dark skin, hair and eye color, she resembles him. She tells everyone she is Japanese. Her mother, who is a Caucasian with light skin, is convinced she needs to explain to her daughter that she is also a white person. Helping a five-year-old understand she is both Caucasian and Asian poses a challenge because not all of her genetic indicators are visibly apparent.

So it is with Jesus' Kingdom and its presence in Timothy's life. It's real, it's a fact, yet it cannot be seen in his physical characteristics. But the Kingdom can and will be seen in his life as he learns to live as a citizen of Jesus' Kingdom and experiences benefits of Kingdom thinking, behavior and lifestyle.

The testimony also communicates about being a new person, spiritually born, who now can begin to see the Kingdom of God. The verse I think about is in the Lord's Prayer: "Thy Kingdom come, thy will be done on earth as it is in heaven." We pray, asking God that we would experience the "Kingdom" here on earth, just as in heaven. Although we still wrestle with sin here, we can have the same attitudes and understanding as those who are in heaven, where there is no sin. The "will" of God can be the same here for us as believers as it is for those in heaven.

Many religious cultures give the impression that after accepting Christ, a person then must get involved in church. Sometimes that is effective, but many times the new believer gets caught up in the programs, jobs and business of the church. For them it becomes an organization rather than an organism. They don't get discipled and don't understand they have been transformed, taken out of the world and put into the Kingdom of God here on earth. They need to understand this is an eternal Kingdom and that someday, in the flash of an eye, all believers will be taken from this earth to the heavenly Kingdom. A testimony about Jesus is a living, ongoing story that I live out and can share whenever the opportunity presents itself – a formal presentation, a group setting, or one-on-one. This story tells about God giving me an undivided heart that puts Him first in all things. He has given me a new Spirit that understands Him. He replaced my heart of stone with new heart that can love Him and others. Now I want to follow his decrees and obey His laws. I know that He is my God and that I am His man.

### Timothy's story

The development of my own personal testimony has been a work in progress since I first invited Christ into my life more than 27 years ago. It began as a simple story of brokenness and a need for God to fill the void in my life at age 40. Writing my first account of this event took place because a formal study required me to write my testimony. It caused me to realize that one particular morning the third chapter of the Gospel of

John had convicted me to confess my sin and invite Jesus into my life as Savior and receive Him as Lord.

Later I was asked by my Paul to give my testimony at a men's retreat. I had plenty of experience talking before a group, but this particular presentation for some reason caused me to feel anxious. Since I had created an outline of what I was planning to say, I thought I could just "wing it" in front of the group. I am not sure exactly what I said, but all of a sudden something choked me up and brought tears to my eyes.

My Paul kept arranging opportunities for me to give my story before groups. Then I began getting invitations to go out of town and share my testimony at larger events with more people in attendance. I put the story into my computer so I could adapt it for different situations and print it out. As I began discipling other men I was able to coach them in developing their own testimony stories. I worked to improve my speaking skills, and God allowed plenty of interesting situations in my life – business failures, health problems and legal problems – that made for interesting storytelling.

Being able to share my testimony with others is one thing that has given me great pleasure over the years. I have a written version I often send via email whenever the opportunity presents itself. Over the years I have rewritten it a number of times, each time updating this ongoing love story of Jesus' Kingdom in my life as it continues to be played out, the most important aspect of my life.

## *Scripture references*
1 John 5:11-13; Romans 3:23; Romans 6:23; 1 Corinthians 15:1-5; John 3:3; 13:1-5; Galatians 2:20; Matthew 6:9-10; 1 John 2:15-16; Matthew 5:16; Ezekiel 11:19-20; John 3:3-21

## *Questions for reflection or discussion*

What are your comments on this chapter?

What has been your personal experience with this topic?

Any Scriptures or principles discussed in this chapter you need to apply in your life?

# 39.
# Lifestyle Evangelism

·······················································

*"When I am with those who are weak, I share their weakness,*
*for I want to bring the weak to Christ. Yes, I try to find common*
*ground with everyone, doing everything I can to save some."*
*1 Corinthians 9:22 (New Living Translation)*

## *Paul's perspective*

The idea of evangelism, presenting the good news of the forgiveness of sin through Jesus Christ to those who have not received it, is a topic that should have considerable interest for Timothy. Many men are timid when it comes to presenting the gospel of salvation to others. They come under the attack of our spiritual enemy, who uses his considerable deceptions and resources to discourage the presentation of the Gospel to the lost.

In 1 Corinthians 9, which I regard as one of the best chapters in the Bible on evangelism, the apostle Paul said he became like those that he was not like. He walked alongside them with Christ, becoming as they were to establish common ground as a platform from which he could share the Gospel. This idea is foreign in our culture today because of the isolation that has often developed that can separate the Christian from those outside of Christ. It is up to the Christian to bridge this gap, to cross over and reach out to the non-believer who is not in Christ.

All effective evangelism is done by God. He is called "the hound of heaven." He is the one who moves into the life of the non-believer, often using the believer to serve as a doorman, opening the entrance into His work. He allows us the privilege of participating with Him as we live in Christ, are willing to engage in prayer for those that don't believe, and live our lives around non-believers so they can experience, through us, the *music* of the Gospel.

Joe Aldrich, in his book, *Lifestyle Evangelism,* says, "The life of the believer is the *music* of the Gospel." Many people in our culture have heard the Gospel but never heard the *music* of the Gospel, which is the emotional side, the love song of God to those He is calling. They have not been loved by anyone and have never seen or experienced the music of a life filled with the fruit of the Holy Spirit. That fruit, the Scriptures tell us, is love, joy, peace, patience, kindness, goodness, faithfulness, gentleness and self-control. When people get close enough to a person who has this fruit – to see it, observe it, experience it, and ask questions about it – they are able to hear and feel the Gospel's *music* and develop a desire to have what the Christian possesses and experiences.

There is a great divide between the Christian and non-Christian in our culture, and many Christians are not willing to venture into the enemy territory and live there, seeking lost souls. A short poem by an unknown author, however, captures the importance of this need very well: "I would rather see a sermon than hear one any day, I would rather one would walk with me, than merely point the way." I think many believers are willing to tell the lost how to find Jesus, but quite unwilling to walk beside them along the way.

People in our culture born prior to 1960 grew up in a culture that was characterized by Judeo-Christian moral values. They heard the Gospel from parents, relatives, and friends, at church and even through the media. The strategy then employed by Christians was simply to present the Gospel when contact was made with non-believers. Because they had heard the message before at some point, the timing would often be right for them to receive and believe this good news. It has been estimated that acceptance of Christ as Savior usually comes, on the average, about the seventh time the person heard the gospel of salvation, so during that time many people had already heard it repeatedly.

However, in the generations born following 1960, during which society has become transformed into post Judeo-Christian culture, many people have had little exposure to Christianity, the Bible or the Gospel. Therefore much cultivation and sowing of the Word is necessary before they are able to grasp the implications of their sin, separation from God, and their need for a Savior. Evangelism has had to change in its form, from an event often labeled as "contact evangelism," to a process that has been termed "lifestyle evangelism." In this newer approach, I no longer expect to share the Gospel with a non-believer until I have prayed for him and invested considerable time in my relationship with him. It takes time for him to get to know me and trust me. This might happen within a few months or take twenty years or more; it all depends on the individual. Regardless of the time, I continue to befriend him, gradually exposing to him what faith in Jesus Christ looks like, along with the peace and joy that dwell within me.

An old saying, "curiosity killed the cat," can be applied to the one-on-one process that takes place between me and the non-believer with whom I am cultivating a relationship. Curiosity is developed by not giving him all the answers. He becomes curious, even baffled, by what I let him see God doing in my life. As his soul awakens, his heart begins longing to see the reality of God in his own life. He is becoming a seeker. This process is known as cultivation, which begins to remove the hard rocks so that the seed can be planted.

At some point I will invite him to start looking at the Scriptures using the *Operation Timothy* process. This is the beginning of sowing the Word of God into his heart. Over time his spiritual roadblocks gradually are cast aside and his heart opens to God's love for him through Christ. The harvest of his soul is in God's control and timing, occurring when He wills for it to take place.

Allow me to share an illustration from my life. A tennis friend, after he had accepted Christ, shared with me that observing how I handled my son's problems with drugs and alcohol had influenced him. He recalled me telling him that everything was going to be fine with my son because of this relationship I had with God. He observed my trust that God would bring my son through these problems. Influenced by how he saw God working in my life, my friend began thinking how he might also surrender some of his problems to God. In this way, an important step in the process was opened up for him as he moved forward in his spiritual journey.

As I open my life up to a man and he begins to see that we have many of the same problems in common, it becomes clear there is not very much difference between our lives. We both have trials and similar struggles. I have to trust God that He will bring the seeker through the process of lifestyle evangelism and give him a willingness to look at the Bible with me. My role with Timothy is to model lifestyle evangelism for him, encouraging him to be proactive with people just as I am proactive.

Timothy and I become active observers of people as we choose to participate in God's work of reconciling men to Himself.

## Timothy's story

I was won into the Kingdom through the principles of lifestyle evangelism at the age of 39. Up until that time I had run into many well-meaning but ill-equipped Christians. Their method of evangelism was to try to connect with me spiritually, usually by inviting me to church or trying to draw me into a conversation about God. But I was spiritually dead. So when their offer was declined, they would walk away, deciding to have nothing more to do with me.

However, I met a man who understood and practiced lifestyle evangelism. He began building a relationship with me based on things that interested me. He would discuss the items I wanted to discuss, worldly matters like sports, business, and current events. It quickly became apparent that there was something different about this man. When I asked him about it, he informed me the difference was his personal relationship with Jesus Christ. This intrigued me. I began to examine his life even more closely.

In the past I had played a game called "Stump the Christian." Perhaps you've played it. It goes like this: "Yeah, if there is a God, why are there starving children in the world?" I found that Christians would begin to defend their God in the face of such questioning. Although I did not believe in God, I instinctively knew if God existed He would not need us to defend Him. Yet, it was different this time. This man of God refused to take the bait to be drawn into defending his God. He would respond by saying, "I don't pretend to have all the answers, but you will stand before God some day and when you do, you can ask Him." Wow, this made the hairs on the back of my neck stand up!

Over a period of six months or so, he stayed connected with me. In spite of my coarse language, crude jokes and attempts to discredit his God, he refused to go away. One thing that really caught my attention was that he would never talk about Jesus unless I brought Him up. When I was done, he was done. Unlike other Christians I had come into contact with, he seemed to have no agenda. He wasn't trying to fix me; he just wanted to be my friend.

Then one day he asked if I would be interested in studying the Bible with him. That was something I had never even considered. In my mind the Bible was nothing more than a dusty, out-of-date book written thousands of years ago that had absolutely no relevance to what was happening today. However, out of respect for his friendship, I agreed.

Mission accomplished. He had done his job. The ultimate goal of lifestyle evangelism is to build a relationship with a person so that, at some point and time, if for no other reason than respect for the friendship, they will agree to look at the Holy Scriptures. We are not responsible for convincing anyone of the truth in the Bible. That is the work of the Holy Spirit. Our job is just to get them into the Word.

Getting into the Word is where lifestyle evangelism can shift into one-on-one discipleship. It only took a couple of months studying God's Word, with my Paul walking alongside me, before I chose to invite Jesus into my life as Lord and Savior. My Paul continues to walk with me today. He has become my spiritual father, imparting to me the vision of winning the lost through lifestyle evangelism.

## Scripture references

1 Corinthians 9:19-22; John 1:12; Galatians 5:22-23; I Peter 3:15; 2 Timothy 2:25-26

. . . . . . . . . . . . . . . . . . . . . . . . . . . . . . . . . . . . . . . . . . . . . . . . . . . . . . . . . . . . . . . . . . . . . . . . . .

## Questions for reflection or discussion

. . . . . . . . . . . . . . . . . . . . . . . . . . . . . . . . . . . . . . . . . . . . . . . . . . . . . . . . . . . . . . . . . . . . . . . . . .

What are your comments on this chapter?

What has been your personal experience with this topic?

Any Scriptures or principles discussed in this chapter you need to apply in your life?

# 40.
# Physical Health
....................................

*"Don't you know that you yourselves are*
*God's temple and that God's Spirit lives in you?"*
*1 Corinthians 3:16*

## Paul's perspective

At some point in the JPT (Jesus, Paul, Timothy) discipleship process the stewardship of Timothy's health will surface. God has given him a body for the purpose of Christ and for the Holy Spirit living out the life of Christ in and through Timothy. Getting an understanding of being a living, breathing advertisement for Christ is a challenge for him to understand and for me to model. Because our bodies are for the use of God in His plan to reveal Himself to mankind, it becomes important for us to take care of our physical bodies.

The apostle Paul speaks to the challenge of offering our bodies as a living sacrifice for God. Timothy and I, like athletes, are in training for the cause of Christ, and our bodies are the vessels God is using to carry out His ministry of reconciliation to the lost world.

Timothy may be a man very mature in the handling of his health and exercising good judgment in affairs of life related to his health. On the other hand, he may be a couch potato who is exercising poor, foolish judgment in how he cares for his physical well-being. Usually he is somewhere in between these two extremes.

It is my job to be a role model for wisdom and good sense with regard to caring for my body. I choose to be neither a zealot nor a sloth, since extremes are seldom appealing to most men. With the demands of family and work, the time and effort needed to maintain a healthy lifestyle often take a back seat. The majority of men by mid-life are living a lifestyle of poor health choices, leading to a rapid decline of their bodies.

As illness and other physical problems emerge, they become concerned. They also may be faced with significant medical costs.

Sadly we live in a culture where many are overweight and out of shape. Fad diets and exercise equipment are big business. For me, maintaining good physical health includes a balanced diet with three healthy meals a day that include all three basic food groups: carbohydrates, protein and fats. Also, modest portions of food, cooked in a healthy manner, along with healthy snacks in between meals. I work out in the gym twice a week. My weight loss goals are set for a period of a year, rather than weeks or a month as many diets promote. It has been said, "Slow and steady wins the race." Weight lost slowly stays off; pounds lost quickly usually return.

There's a very clear spiritual benefit for physical health. A healthy body has a better chance of overcoming the evil one. When I am tired, out of shape, and not taking care of myself, the evil one has a better venue for entering into my life and affecting my spiritual well-being. Jesus commanded us to love ourselves as we also love our neighbors. Loving *me* has to do with taking care of myself – and not abusing myself. Attacks from the evil one can harm me even to the point where I am unable to overcome the harm he has done. So without question, the physical aspect of my life is very important to the spiritual aspect of my life.

I find healthy living gives me pleasure. It's important for me to have a recreational outlet. Golf, tennis and fishing are popular ones for me. Times away from the cares of the world are important to health. Enjoying recreational activities with my Timothy is a very important part of the discipleship process. Getting alongside of him in an activity rather than always across the table from him is vital. Our world is full of pleasure-giving temptations. On the other hand, dogmatically denying myself any pleasure, whether it involves food, exercise, or recreation, is unhealthy, even weird for me. So moderation with recreation is important to avoid getting out of balance, resulting in not having time for other important aspects of my life.

Some men are very neglectful of their health care. When a man is young and healthy, this might work, but as he ages, this behavior begins to catch up with him. Foolish behavior, if not promptly attended to, can lead to more serious complications. My father, a frugal man, lost two young sisters in his youth to tuberculosis due to the lack of timely, effective health care. Because of this, he insisted that I be a good steward of my health and was not miserly with our health care money. I can think of no better investment than money spent on effective health care – especially prevention.

Our bodies serve as the battleground for the war that goes on within our soul. It's the battle between the Spirit and the sinful nature. The flesh, where the sinful nature resides, cannot obey God's Word or please God. It has no desire to do so. I have the choice to let the Spirit control my mind or to let the sinful nature have control over me. Through Christ and His Spirit, I have been released from the control the old nature used to have over me. I am free to choose my master. I want my body to be a healthy vessel for the Holy Spirit to live in, leading me, and bringing glory and honor to God.

## *Timothy's story*

I grew up in an athletic environment playing sports like basketball, baseball, football and track. My life after college revolved around sports that I was coaching. My recreations included golf, tennis, surfing, snow skiing, swimming and scuba diving. In addition, I used weightlifting, jogging and stretching to keep myself healthy.

Entering my 30's, however, I began to notice my body was in a state of decline. Exercise became more painful and the recovery took longer. With each passing year my weight began to be harder to control. I quit smoking and started slowly limiting my use of alcohol. This was not easy, since my flesh had ruled in these areas for much of my life. As I aged I became dissatisfied with my life and the decline of my physical health.

At age 40 I discovered my spiritual depravity, which led me to a relationship with Jesus. As I read and studied the Bible, I discovered that Jesus cared for me and wanted me to keep my body healthy for His use.

About this time, I met my Paul. He was modeling a healthy physical lifestyle of moderation. He enjoyed healthy living and we often enjoyed recreation together with tennis and golf. My Paul told me about how his own Paul had allowed himself to get out of shape and become unhealthy. He lived to be 87, but by the time he was 70 his health decline had taken him out of an active part in the ministry. I did not want this to happen to me. I continued to work at a healthy lifestyle for the next 18 years. This paid off with good health, strength and energy for maintaining a balanced lifestyle of marriage, family, work and ministry.

At 63, I was finally getting my act together, ready for the next 15 to 20 years of great productivity with my one-on-one ministry to men. I now had more than 20 years of experience in ministry, and 40-plus years of experience in marriage, business and work. My finances were in great shape, and physically I was healthy, with excellent energy and strength for opportunities that would come my way.

However, God had a different plan for me. I experienced a pain in my right rib cage area and shortness of breath. In the emergency room I was diagnosed with a pulmonary embolism, a blood clot in my lung. After eight days in the hospital I began experiencing a new phase of life that involved numerous attacks on my physical health.

The good news is the years I spent taking care of my body with exercise, recreation and moderate eating habits had paid off. I have been able to continue these disciplines and stay in the battle for the souls of men. God has provided the strength I need to plow through the afflictions, fight a good fight, keep the faith and finish the race.

God has allowed me to experience health issues for His reasons. My relationship with Him has grown through afflictions and struggles. He is using the experiences in my life as I use them as part of my ministry to men. I do not know what plan God has for me in the future, but trust He will provide the strength to use my body effectively for His ministry, in and through me.

## Scripture references

1 Corinthians 3:16; Colossians 2:9,10,12; Romans 12:1; Matthew 22:38-39; Romans 8:6-8; Romans 7:6; 1 Corinthians 4:19-20; Job 2:3-7; 2 Timothy 4:7; 1 Chronicles 16:9a: Zephaniah 17:3

## *Questions for reflection or discussion*

What are your comments on this chapter?

What has been your personal experience with this topic?

Any Scriptures or principles discussed in this chapter you need to apply in your life?

# 41.
# Male Sexuality

·······································

*"Now for the matters you wrote about: It is good for a man not to marry. But since there is so much immorality, each man should have his own wife and each woman her own husband. The husband should fulfill his marital duty to his wife, and likewise the wife to her husband. The wife's body does not belong to her alone but also to her husband. In the same way, the husband's body does not belong to him alone but also to his wife. Do not deprive each other except by mutual consent and for a time, so that you may devote yourselves to prayer. Then come together again so that Satan will not tempt you because of your lack of self-control."*
*1 Corinthians 7:1-5*

## *Paul's perspective*

Discipling Timothy presents a unique challenge when helping him in the area of his male sexuality. The improper handling of this area in Timothy's life leads into debilitating sin, both inside and outside of marriage. A few men I discipled have chosen to remain unmarried and celibate. But they are the exception. Most men have a wife – or are looking for one.

A man's sexual relationship with his wife is often a touchy subject, making it difficult for him to be transparent in this area. When the time is right, the best way to open the subject with the man is to share the story about my own sexuality with him. Eventually the man has to be able to communicate honestly with his wife about what it is like for him to deal with his lustful temptations. He has to be open and transparent, without getting emotional – or defensive.

Many men get married so they can have a woman with whom their sexual needs are met – so that they won't have to go to multiple women to satisfy their need. I have met with a number of Christian men who married for this reason, but when their wife did not meet their need, they went outside the marriage to someone else to get satisfied. The husband's need is often not understood or communicated well to the wife. Her unwillingness to accept the man's need and see it through his eyes can be used by Satan to ruin relationships and break up marriages.

Every woman needs to have an understanding of male sexuality, especially with younger men coming up through today's culture. They think that sex and love automatically exist together. It is a rude awakening when men discover that it takes two to make this a reality. When a woman understands and meets her husband's need, it is a testimony of her love and acceptance of him. This can be a huge factor in bringing God into the center of their lives, as well as the lives of their children.

Some men have made themselves available to just about any women that came across their path. Healing for a man like this involves choosing to enjoy one sexual partner exclusively for the rest of his life, instead of having multiple sexual relationships. As he grows with Christ, his life will take a new direction and he's enabled to live a new life. He will learn to allow one woman to meet his sexual needs by trusting that God is aware of that need and will meet it through her.

This is similar to the sobriety of an alcoholic who abstained from drinking; the male abstains from multiple sex relationships, learning to be content with having his sexual needs met through one woman, learning and experiencing the fulfillment of meeting her sexual needs. One drink for the alcoholic can lead to circumstances that bring chaos and disorder to his life. So it is with the male going outside the marriage to get his needs met. It too will result in chaos and disorder, many times culminating in the destruction of the marriage and the family.

For many people in the Christian realm, the idea of just looking at another woman is regarded as sin, which creates a lot of unnecessary guilt among Christian men. I don't see any problem with men observing the attractiveness of women and noticing that they are well-constructed. The problem begins when a man lets his mind dwell on what having sex with that woman might be like. Satan is always using this kind of situation to tempt men, but temptation is common to all men – and it is not sin. If I allow my mind to dwell on another woman, and especially if I chase after her, then I have entered into serious sexual sin.

We live with women; they are everywhere, and many of them are very appealing to the eye. In our culture they dress provocatively; if we go to a pool or the beach, many of them wear just enough clothing to make themselves more interesting. When wives see us constantly looking at other women, whether at dinner, sporting events or socials, it breeds insecurity in our relationships with them. Our wives have a great need to feel from us that they are the only women that can meet our needs.

We learn to live with this as followers of Christ and not allow the temptations that confront us to move into sin. Healing from sexual pre-occupation and addiction does not mean being a "holy Joe," walking around with a self-righteous hat on in this area. It is living as a fallen man and allowing Christ to take over. This will allow me to walk through life not in sexual bondage, but free to live by the Spirit of God in the area of sexual temptation.

Being a Paul, involved in discipling other men for 33 years, I have met with a number of them that have been wounded by sexual addictions. I have been walking alongside one particular Timothy for six years. As we were sitting at Starbucks one Saturday morning, a few days after he had turned his life over to Jesus Christ, he spoke with me in tears of his marriage of 25 years. He had engaged in multiple affairs, and was currently in an affair that had lasted for nine years. He now was a new creature in Christ, but felt on the brink of losing his wife and relationships with his three grown children.

At that point, despite still being "in love" with his mistress, he returned to his wife and asked her forgiveness. She chose to stay in the marriage, and little by little God has been restoring them. As this Timothy walks with Christ, who strengthens him, he is able to turn his heart back to his wife.

But the restoration has not been without many painful experiences. He would often say to his daughter, "Don't let any man bring you down." One day she reminded him of that and said, "Dad, I never thought *you* would be the man that would bring me down." He has made his wife a priority, and God is restoring his family. Now, five years later and after much healing from God, he has begun to meet with other men going through problems similar to those God has walked him through.

Another man was an engineer with a wife and two daughters. We had been in the midst of a nine-year discipling relationship when we took a trip together and were discussing a ministry opportunity I thought would be a good fit for him. He turned to me and stated, "You don't really know me; I could never do anything like that."

Surprised, I asked him what it was I didn't know. He told me that whenever his wife left town, he would rent X-rated videos and enjoy the pleasure of that sexual experience. He told me how ashamed he was. He had not communicated this secret with another human. I told him that I had those kinds of trials myself, and that God had healed me when I got the truth out in the open and talked about it. He prayed with me and we asked God to heal him. God answered. He took the ministry opportunity and was very fruitful for the kingdom of God. He has also become a man that is meeting one-on-one with other men.

Unwinding a man's sexual background often represents a difficult challenge. Unhealthy male sexuality generally becomes an addiction, and without God to heal the addiction, it seems like a hopeless task to overcome it. Openness with regard to Timothy's male sexuality is a subject where I must be willing to go with him so God can lead him out of unhealthy sexual behavior and free him to become the man the Lord wants him to be.

## Timothy's story

I grew up as the oldest of three boys in a home where our dad was an alcoholic. Developing a healthy outlook on sex was next to impossible. My training came from what felt good, and from listening to my friends and their experiences. Entering the high school years, we were all sexually active; probably 75 percent of our conversations were about girls. We talked about the ones we thought looked the best and the ones we thought were most available. Our goal was to conquer the ones that we could. The final stage was bringing the tales of the conquest back to the group for evaluation.

When I joined the Air Force at the age of 17, I continued this behavior that had turned into my life purpose. There were days that I would burn with lust, whenever my need was somehow delayed. At 24, I married a 17-year-old because she had become pregnant with my child. I felt it was the right thing to do. But I brought my addiction with me into my marriage and was caught in adultery a couple of times. I lived with threats that I would be beaten with a baseball bat while I was sleeping.

This terrible relationship ended when I was 32 years old, after it had produced two children. I was now single and had accumulated some financial resources – my cars, boats, second homes and cash. They were all very helpful in finding new prey. At 35, I married for the second time, moved in with my new wife with all my sex toys, Playboys, pornographic movies, etc. My fear going into the marriage was that I would not be able to sustain a relationship with just one woman.

My second wife worked for a man that called himself a Christian businessman. He encouraged us to read the Bible, which we did. I became very attracted to the person of Jesus Christ. I read that He had died for sinners, and I identified with His payment for my sin. In due time found peace with God and realized that God loved me and desired a relationship with me.

Over the next eight years, little by little, Christ began to heal me. I am thankful for my Paul's encouragement and prayers for me. God used a healthy relationship with another man to show me His love, which is what I needed. I am very thankful to God for His healing of this addiction. I am also thankful for my wife and her patience with me. My sexual needs have been met by one woman – my wife – for many years now. The "burning lust" is no longer a part of my life, but I will never forget it, nor the suffering that it caused me and others.

## Scripture references

1 Corinthians 7:1-5; 1 Corinthians 7:8, 9; 1 John 2:15, 16; Romans 7:6; Ephesians 5:3-4; Acts 15:29; Hebrews 13:4; Philippians 4:13; 1 Corinthians 10:13; 1 John 1:9

## Questions for reflection or discussion

What are your comments on this chapter?

What has been your personal experience with this topic?

Any Scriptures or principles discussed in this chapter you need to apply in your life?

# A Final Word

.......................................

*"May the Lord direct your hearts into*
*God's love and Christ's perseverance."*
*2 Thessalonians 3:5*

The apostle John writes his ending to the Gospel of John by declaring, "Jesus in the three short years of his ministry on earth did many other things that if every one of them were written down the whole world would not have room for the books that would be written." While there is much more that could be said regarding the subject of "imitating" Paul in the discipleship process, and ultimately Jesus Christ, there is not enough to fill up the whole world with books. But at the same time, these chapters only scratch the surface. Entire books have been written about many of the individual topics that the preceding chapters have addressed. The intent of the book is not to be exhaustive on any of those subjects, but to be a resource for and cast vision on the Jesus, Paul, Timothy (JPT) relationship.

If you are a mature believer and feel you could help another person, you could seek out a man into whom you could impart your life. Or, if you are in need of being discipled, you could seek out a Paul to come alongside of you and impart his life with Christ to you. This JPT process is a way to help another person learn to walk with Christ and mature in Him.

So I'm wholeheartedly encouraging you, the reader, to get into the life of another by meeting, talking and praying about the meaningful aspects of your life.

*"We loved you so much that we were delighted to share with you not only the Gospel of God but our lives as well, because you had become so dear to us"* (1 Thessalonians 2:8).

# Appendix I

......................................

## *Contrasting Mentoring and Discipleship*

[Assumes all relationships are one-on-one as Teacher/Student vs. Paul/Timothy]

| MENTORING/COACHING | vs. | DISCIPLESHIP |
|---|---|---|
| **Relationship Contrasts** | | |
| Friend | vs. | Family |
| Next door neighbor | vs. | Parent |
| A sage advisor | vs. | A follower and a pupil |
| Affection | vs. | Love |
| It's a short-term commitment | vs. | Lifetime commitment |
| Teaching | vs. | Walking through life |
| Program or a process | vs. | A process |
| Teachers and students | vs. | Co-laborers |
| Degrees of relationships varies | vs. | Relationship with Jesus foremost |
| Mentee following mentor | vs. | Modeling the following of Christ |
| Helpful attitude | vs. | Life or death attitude |
| **Authority Contrasts** | | |
| Selectively following advice | vs. | Obedience to God's Word |
| Teacher is the authority | vs. | Christ is the authority |
| Varied value systems | vs. | Eternal value system |
| Plan varies | vs. | Biblical plan |

| Teacher exhibits strength | vs. | Teacher and student exhibit weakness |
|---|---|---|
| Student exhibits weakness | vs. | Dependency on Christ |

### Behavior Contrasts

| If it makes sense do it | vs. | Follow me and do as I do |
|---|---|---|
| No example necessary | vs. | Example is necessary |
| What you do does not affect me | vs. | What you do affects me |
| Advice and control | vs. | Responsibility and accountability |
| I don't necessarily live what I say | vs. | I live what I say |
| Participating requires skill | vs. | Participants required to be faithful, available and teachable |
| Variety of acceptable learning situations | vs. | Face to face in the flesh |
| Reactive | vs. | Proactive |
| Promotes pride | vs. | Promotes humility |

### Result Contrasts

| This may help me | vs. | I am responsible to disciple others [4th generation reproduction] |
|---|---|---|
| Not necessarily any world vision | vs. | World vision |
| Pointing in a direction | vs. | Pointing to Christ as the direction |
| Focused on personal growth | vs. | Focused on spiritual growth in the context of life situations |
| Counting the costs is optional | vs. | Counting the costs with vision, planning and discipline |

| | | |
|---|---|---|
| Purpose of personal maturity | vs. | Purpose of maturity in Christ |
| Prosperity is the expected result | vs. | Discipline and pruning are the expected results |
| Witness for various agenda's | vs. | Witness for the Gospel of Christ |
| Yielded to various agenda's | vs. | Yielded to God and used by Him |
| Issues may or may not be superficial | vs. | Involved in the gut issues of life |
| Focus varies | vs. | Focused on character, community and competency |
| Focused on teaching theories | vs. | Focused on how to trust God |
| Temporal investment | vs. | Eternal Investment |
| Mentor expects results | vs. | Disciple expects nothing in return |
| People need to find themselves | vs. | People need to lose one's self for Christ's sake |

# Appendix II

In the Gospel of Matthew, chapter 13, Jesus talks about what the Kingdom of God is like. He does not define it but describes it. He says it is with you here, even though we cannot see, feel or touch it. Jesus tells us we can translate ourselves from being a person only, to being born again, thus becoming a person of the Kingdom.

The disciples ask Jesus why He is speaking in parables. He explains they had been given the ability to know the mysteries of the Kingdom of heaven. Those who do not have the Kingdom see, but they do not see; they hear, but they do not hear. What has been given to them will be taken away from them. Blessed are those who hear and see.

In verse 22, the so-called Parable of the Sower, Jesus says that when anyone hears the Word of the Kingdom and doesn't understand it, the wicked one comes and snatches it away. In verse 24, Jesus explains the Kingdom of Heaven is like a man who sows good seed in his field and while he slept his enemy came and sowed tares among good seed. When the grain sprouted, the tares also appeared. In this story He is showing us how the seeds of the Kingdom grow in the midst of the world around us.

In verse 31, Jesus states the Kingdom is like a mustard seed, planted in a field. In verse 33, the Kingdom is described as yeast mixed in with the dough as bread is made. And in verse 44, it is compared to a treasure hidden in a field that a man found and used to buy a field. The Kingdom in verse 45 is likened to a merchant who finds one pearl more beautiful than all the others, so he sells all he has so he can go and buy that pearl. Finally, a fishing net is also used in verse 47 to describe the Kingdom.

The book of Matthew speaks of the Kingdom, and the study of it will enlighten us. A lot of this study reveals for us the future of the Kingdom – what it will look like so we can consider the things of the Kingdom that will follow the present time. These are wonderful things to think about and meditate on.

# Appendix III

## Building Community

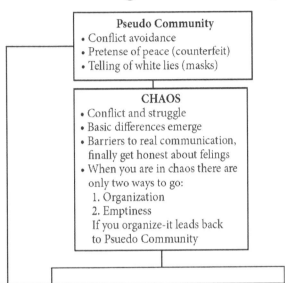

**Pseudo Community**
- Conflict avoidance
- Pretense of peace (counterfeit)
- Telling of white lies (masks)

**CHAOS**
- Conflict and struggle
- Basic differences emerge
- Barriers to real communication, finally get honest about felings
- When you are in chaos there are only two ways to go:
  1. Organization
  2. Emptiness
  If you organize-it leads back to Psuedo Community

**ORGANIZATION**

Three types:
1. **Fixers**    Fix all problems
2. **Sellers**    Try to convert their way of thinking
3. **Dictators**    Impose peace

**EMPTINESS**

Examine self:
1. Preconceptions/expectations
2. Prejudices
3. Ideology and theology
4. Need to heal, convert, control
5. Death has to occur here (primarily death to **self**)

**COMMUNITY**
Open, vulnerable Loving, acceptance

Form follows function

## Practical Tips

☆ Never judge or place value on others' comments, ideas

☆ Speak in first person

☆ Don't try to fix

☆ Listen attentively

☆ Don't quit in chaos

☆ Learn to die to self

# Appendix IV

..................................

## One Man

God brought mankind into existence through "one man," Adam. Since the fall of Adam and Eve, God has been relentlessly pursuing and drawing individual men into a relationship with Him for His purpose. When God asked "Adam, where are you?" (Genesis 3:9), after he chose to sin, God continued to pursue Adam in spite of the fact he had chosen to disobey Him.

God's use of one man moves on to Noah and then to Abraham, the one man whose family was the instrument God used to begin His work and reveal Himself to Abraham's kin. The truth that Abraham learned he imparted to his son, Isaac, and Isaac imparted it to his son, Jacob, who was renamed Israel by God (Genesis 32:28). From his sons the nation of Israel was born, God again using one man.

All of Israel's family was now in Egypt and numbered 70 (Exodus 1:5). That generation all died there, but the Israelites were fruitful and multiplied greatly; they became exceedingly numerous and Egypt was filled with them (Exodus 1:7). Then God called another man, Moses (Exodus 1:3). He was greatly used by God in a miraculous way to free the Israelites from slavery in Egypt. Moses discipled Joshua, and God tells Joshua that as He was with Moses, so He would be with him, as he is used to bring the Israelites back to the Promised Land (Joshua 1:5).

This model proceeds into the judges, the prophets and the kings. God makes His statements and brings about restoration by using men to impart His will to others. In 2 Kings 2:2 Elijah said to Elisha, "Stay here, for the Lord has sent me to Bethel." Elisha replied, "As surely as the Lord lives and you live, I will not leave you." So they went down to Bethel. Elijah had been Elisha's godly discipler and he was staying with him, regardless of the cost. This relationship illustrates the heart of man-to-man discipleship. As men, we tend to look at the outward appearance, but God looks at the heart of a man (1 Samuel 16:7).

Have you ever considered asking God for a heart like the seer spoke of to King Asa in 2 Chronicles 16:9? "For the eyes of the Lord search to and fro throughout the whole earth to find a heart that is perfect toward Him." This seems to be what God is looking for. When this happens in a man, God begins to give him what He himself inherits: "men." He says that His portion is His people (Deuteronomy. 32:9), so He begins giving people to us. For most of us, as businessmen, it is a difficult transition to genuinely believe that reward from God is truly connected with people and helping them to connect with Him one person at a time. He gives us people because we are precious to Him (Isaiah. 43:4), then he begins to reveal to us individually the true meaning of our life in Christ.

Spiritual concepts must be learned by faith. For example, Jesus Christ said that if we follow Him, we will become fishers of men (Matthew 4:19). Paul said that he loved those he ministered to so much that he was willing to give his life for them (1 Thessalonians 2:8).

When I was a kid, any time there was a ball game of any kind, I was ready. As an adult, I've concluded this is God's game: finding men, helping them get connected to Him, then walking alongside them as they learn to get in the same game I am playing (1 Corinthians 4:15-16). An extremely meaningful life is wrapped up in this endeavor. This book has been written to help us all better understand this calling where God uses "one man" to accomplish some of His work and plans in another man.

*– Dave Rathkamp*

# Appendix V

......................

## Discipling the Secular Man

The following are <u>Intentional Strategic Steps for the One-on One Discipleship Process</u>

1. The discipler, dependent upon God, prays asking Him for a loving heart for the lost, secular man that God sends him.
2. The discipler befriends the secular man. (This can take one minute or many years, using Lifestyle Evangelism principles.)
3. The discipler (who becomes his Paul) investigates the credibility of the Bible with him (using Book One of *Operation Timothy*).
4. As the man meets with his Paul, led by the Holy Spirit, he begins to trust God, believes the Word, and receives Jesus Christ as his Lord and Savior. (This step involves reading the Gospels. Suggesting a *Life Application Bible* with commentaries would be helpful.)
5. In this next step, as he becomes my Timothy, he develops basic familiarity with the Bible (meeting with Paul using Books 2-4 of *Operation Timothy*).
6. He then makes a decision to identify with Christ daily and be His disciple. This becomes evident as he is:
   (a) a committed follower of Christ (loving Him more than his career, position, power, prestige and material things).
   (b) committed to applying the Word to his life (hearing, reading, studying, memorizing and meditating on Scripture).
   (c) committed to be a witness for Christ (developing an effective Gospel testimony).
   (d) committed to be a discipler of others (a "2 Timothy 2:2 man") who models:
      (1) consistent quiet time
      (2) active prayer life

(3) intimacy with Christ

(4) fellowship with like-minded men

(5) discipline with: finances, work, family, wife, sex, health

(6) pursues men and commits to disciple them resulting in fruit (spiritual reproduction).

In this discipleship process, the Holy Spirit's fruit in a man results in a **self-initiating, reproducing, fully devoted follower of Christ.**

# About the Authors

**Jay Baker** became a follower of Jesus Christ in 1983 and started meeting with Dave Rathkamp in the one-on-one discipleship process in 1985. He has been in the real estate business in Houston, Texas for 36 years and specializes in the sale of land for the development of residential subdivisions. During his business career, Jay has been involved in the ownership and management of investment properties, a real estate brokerage firm, a bank, and a savings and loan.

A former basketball player and high school coach in Houston, Texas who enjoys playing golf, Jay lives with his wife, Nancy, on a small farm just north of Houston. They have a son, Kelly, a daughter, Kasey, and two granddaughters, Aiden and Jessie.


**Dave Rathkamp** became a follower of Jesus Christ in 1976 in Atlanta, Georgia. It was another businessman that took an interest in him and pointed him toward Christ. After Dave received Christ into his life, Joe Coggeshall sought him out and began discipling him weekly for the next few years. Dave spent 21 years as a teaching tennis professional. He began at The Bath & Tennis Club in Palm Beach Florida and later worked as the director of tennis at the 1,800-member Cherokee Town & Country Club in Atlanta. He moved to Houston in 1981 for the purpose of winning and discipling businessmen.

Dave and his wife, Donna, live in Northwest Houston. Their four children – Royce, Kelley, Laura and Paul – are grown and all live within two miles of their parents. Dave and Donna have ten grandchildren and two great-grandchildren.

To contact the authors, write to:
Imitatemebook2012@gmail.com
You can also visit the website:
www.houston.cbmc.com

Made in the USA
Charleston, SC
21 October 2012